POINTS OF YOU

Four Friends from MIT on Growing Up

Vick Liu
Julia Rue
Mina Fahmi
Drew Bent

To Ben and Stanley,
the inspiration for
this journey.

POINTS

INTRODUCTION

One year ago on a crisp Boston morning, the four of us sat down and decided to write a book together. Other than our friendship, we had very little in common. We had each grown up in different places with different cultures. Our aspirations — to become better engineers, artists, educators, and creators — had little overlap. Some of us were getting into the swing of college, while others were set to graduate. Despite these differences, we all shared an understanding of the challenges that come with growing up, and a desire to connect with others going through the same difficulties.

We decided to write this book to share the lessons we learned and mistakes we made since going through college and growing in life. This book is a collection of thoughts and stories that highlight our experiences, real and unfiltered. Nobody has the answers to life, but we hope that by sharing the perspectives of four very different people, you might find companionship, understanding, and a new point of view.

VICK LIU

Coming out of high school, I felt pretty confident about myself. Frankly, I was pretty full of myself. I thought I had life figured out and that's probably why I felt so off-balance when college came around.

College scared the hell out of me. In high school, I had breezed through most of my classes, but in college, I struggled with a lot of the classes I was taking. I thought I was capable of doing well in a more competitive environment, but my inability to perform made me scared and confused. Outside of class, a new environment, new social groups, easy access to alcohol, and a more casual sexual environment made me reconsider many of the values I had grown up with. I felt the pressure to change slowly begin to surround me.

When Thanksgiving came around my freshman year, I just wanted to run home and hide. I didn't feel ready for the challenges college came with. That break, I sat in my bed and read the books I had enjoyed as a kid. If my parents or my brothers asked me how school was, I would just say that it was going well and I was having a good time. When my family dropped me off at the airport to fly back to school, I almost begged them to let me stay a few more days. I felt overwhelmed at school and sometimes I just wanted to stay in bed all day. More than anything else, I felt that I didn't have anyone to turn to for advice or for help. I'm the eldest of three brothers so I have always been the one offering to help, not the one asking for help.

Looking back, I should have learned to lean on the upperclassmen around me and I should have asked for help when I needed it. I was ashamed I hadn't learned to swim yet in this new environment and a lot of the time, I felt like I was drowning.

If I could go back in time and sit down with my 16 year-old self, these are the stories and the pieces of advice that I would pass on. Growing up, I made a lot of mistakes — some minor and some more serious. With this book, the other authors and I want to share our stories with you. We want to share the mistakes we've made and the lessons we've learned. We want you to know that you are not alone. Everyone goes through their own struggles and we want you to be aware of what's to come. I hope you can walk away from this book with a few things to keep in mind even if it's only an exposure to a new perspective.

JULIA RUE

I have been journaling since the sixth grade. In these journals, I recorded not my life events, but my feelings: simple feelings like sadness and joy and fear, and complex feelings like disappointment and eagerness. Once these feelings were written down, I could pick them apart and look at them upside down, and most importantly, tuck them back away into the unassuming pages of a journal that I swore would never see the eyes of another human being.

When journaling, I feel so rawly human; I feel in touch with both my reasoning and emotions. And through these journals, I waded through the muck of twenty-two years of life and built my current belief and system of understanding.

Earlier this year, Vick showed me a draft of a book he wanted to write and I immediately connected with his writing. In a way, the draft was his own journal. I found the written words so deeply relevant and uncanningly familiar — the struggle to understand why he thought and acted as he did and the exploration on how to think and act differently. I was witnessing his raw humanity, and it was beautiful. My journals were great for helping myself through life, but I realized that sharing my thoughts in a written format would create new beauty for myself and others, by connecting us through untouched thoughts, gut reactions, and deep reflections.

While reading this book, I hope that you find our thought processes interesting. I hope you probe at our analysis and challenge our life axioms. I hope you apply yourself to these stories and let yourself react genuinely. I hope that you inquire why we dare publish these thoughts. And I dream that in this book you find something beautiful.

MINA FAHMI

A couple of years ago in the midst of Boston winter, I became sicker than I'd ever been before. I couldn't eat. The act of sitting upright required unbearable effort. Sleep was my only momentary relief.

When I had been depressed before, I experienced symptoms commonly prescribed: Lack of interest. Anhedonia. Narrow thinking. But this time was more intense. It was as though my body had given up working, coupled to the unshakeable belief that my future was hopeless.

How did things come to this? Since middle school, friends would come to me looking for advice — about relationships, about themselves, about life. I tried to help as best I could, and was told I had a talent for empathy. My greatest happiness was hearing someone say, "You made me feel better."

Despite helping others, I never knew how to fix my own problems. Over the years I developed poor ways of processing my emotions and maintaining relationships with others. I reflect on this without criticism — we all develop weaknesses in life, and grow to improve or accept them. But that winter, my fears, indecision, and isolation came to a peak. Even in this state, I knew deep down that I had to get better.

It's been nearly two years since then, and I'm in a better place than I have ever been. The lessons I learned during this experience, along with those from before and after, transformed and defined who I am today. Change is an unavoidable aspect of life, and the presence of these lessons in my life will no doubt change over time. But today, they are invaluable.

The four of us provide our thoughts not as a book of answers but as the sum total of who we are at this moment in our lives. While writing this book, we focused on capturing things we wish we'd known years ago. It is our hope that these lessons help you feel understood during a particularly confusing time in life, and see a new way of thinking about living.

Years in the future, my thoughts on these topics may change. And if I'd learned what I know now two years ago, there's no way of telling whether I would have had the same challenges. But I do not mind not knowing. I simply hope that this book can be of some value to you, even in a small way.

DREW BENT

I first heard about this project from Vick and couldn't believe it. It seemed absolutely crazy that we as 20-something-year-olds would consider writing a book. Why should anyone listen to us?

But then I scanned through the first 100 thoughts that Vick had left in his journal for his brothers to read one day. And it struck me: there was a certain candidness, humility, and even confusion in his words. It almost felt like I had written them. This was not a book written by people who had already made it and were cherry-picking their favorite stories to share with others. This was a journal — nothing more, nothing less — written by young people, for young people. It was raw and incomplete. It was just like why I'd rather listen to my older sister than some random CEO for advice. It was real.

The point of this book shouldn't be for you to read our words like holy scripture or something. We are going through life just like everyone else. Throughout a number of the sections, we disagree with one another — sometimes vehemently.

Rather, I hope you take this as an opportunity to question your own values and experiences. Every time you read one of our thoughts, it may be helpful to ask yourself, Do I agree with that? Why or why not? If you have the opportunity to write down your own musings as well, go for it. If there's one thing I learned from this project, it's that it's never too early to start documenting our thoughts and values.

CHANGING PERSPECTIVES

Almost everyone has completely valid reasons for their viewpoints in arguments and discussions. Even more important, just because you have a reason that is "right" doesn't mean that the other side must be "wrong".

Sometimes you have an assumption about the world and just decide to run with it. It may not be a correct assumption at the moment, and it may even be a crazy idea to pursue. But by running with it — and inspiring everyone else around you to run with it as well — you may surprise yourself and turn the assumption into reality through sheer persistence and optimism.ⒹⒷ

I can't promise you that every day will be a good day, but I challenge you to always find something positive to smile about even when things aren't so great. Life is too short not to spend everyday smiling and laughing about something even if only for a few seconds.Ⓥ

When dealt with a difficult compromise, the first question you may want to ask is why not try for both options together. Often wanting both is infeasible or even foolish, but the mere act of putting this third option on the table can open your eyes to a whole universe of new alternatives.ⒹⒷ

It hurts more to lose than it feels good to gain. Our minds tend to focus on pain, regret, and failure above blessings and success. Knowing this, we must put in extra effort to be thankful, or risk living life disappointed.🄜🄕

When you're trying hard and struggling to get people to say yes to something, stop and figure out why you want their 'yes' in the first place. Do you really need it? Either you'll find the deeper reason or you'll discover that you don't really need their approval or acknowledgement at all!🄓🄑

Struggling against what you cannot control does nothing but cause more suffering.🄜🄕

As the physicist Richard Feynman and his wife Arline would ask, what do you care what other people think of you? This doesn't mean you should never care, but that you should really dig deep and understand why you care.**DB**

A million thoughts race through our minds every day. Thoughts about the world around us, about ourselves, about the future. If you slow down and observe passing thoughts, you can notice patterns, and in turn learn what is important to you.**MF**

When something or someone out there frustrates you, delve deeper into your feelings. Unless that thing that is frustrating you is yourself, there is nothing really to be frustrated about. See yourself as what you can and should be: a positive influence on what was frustrating you.**DB**

When we dream of the future, our thoughts are filled with hope and possibility. Day-to-day reality is usually never as exciting though. Why is this? It might simply be that we're idealistic. Another option is that we tend to forget all the little discomforts that pile up. Life can be filled with exceptional experiences which are dampened by little and large irritations. But don't forget, the good is still there.⬤

A not-so-bad way of looking at the world is this: you have an incredible amount of control over your future outcomes. Indeed, we all do. Yet when judging the outcomes of your past self and of others, know that they are more likely tied to luck and their environments than anything of their own doing. Such a mindset will keep you ambitious yet grounded. We are in control of our destinies, only until we aren't, in which case we better not take more credit than we deserve.⬤

Whenever I catch a cold and I'm all stuffed up, I wish I could take a calm, deep breath. But I rarely remember to appreciate breathing when I'm feeling well. Even if the whole world is upside down for you right now, and you've got a cold on top of that, try to find something small left to enjoy.🅜🅕

Until I started reading about the conditions of other countries and seeing the pictures myself, I didn't realize just how lucky I am to have a roof over my head, warm food in my stomach, clean water to drink from, and a family that cares for me. Since then, I've started to care less about the extravagant luxuries in life and I have become more thankful for the simple things that I used to take for granted.🆅🇱

If you can, find opportunities to explore an unfamiliar way of life. The summer after my senior year in high school, I spent a few weeks working on a farm in Alaska. To wake up early in the morning and chow down on breakfast before working in the fields, to hitch a ride in the flatbed of a truck to grab lunch, and to spend afternoons chopping wood to fill a stockpile — it was an experience I had only ever read about in my history books. Going through it myself was an entirely new experience and getting to know my hosts, both farmers, was even more delightful. In their community, they traded flowers they grew for freshly baked loaves of bread from one neighbor and freshly made ice cream from trading with another. In this community, good food and conversation were the keys to a fulfilling and happy life. They may not have had as many material possessions as I had observed growing up in LA, but they had a lot more heart, a lot more compassion, and a lot more kindness than anyone I had ever known.🆅🇱

I used to think that the most beautiful things in life were objects you could buy like supercars and fancy houses, but I was also eleven then. After growing older, I've come to realize that the most beautiful things in life are memories — memories of people, places, and feelings. My most cherished possessions are ones you can't take away: memories of pulling pranks with my friends, memories of watching shooting stars race each other across the sky while camping in the desert, memories of the passion in my friend's eyes as she told me about what interested her, memories of road trips with my family.🆅🅛

At the end of high school I had saved enough money to pick up a GoPro camera, and I took it with me everywhere. If I traveled to a new city, sometimes I would see more of the city through the GoPro lens than through my own actual eyes. I was eager to get the perfect shot, to stitch together videos of the different adventures so I could remember all that I had done. I remember one night I was reviewing some of the shots that I had taken. As I made notes about which shots to keep, I marvelled at how beautiful the scenery had been. I also regretted the fact that I had not been able to stop and enjoy the moment with my own eyes because I had gotten so caught up with taking videos of the scenery. I still make videos, but now I'm much more concerned with enjoying the sights myself before even thinking about turning on the camera.🆅🅛

When most people miss something, they want it to come back. Sometimes it can be a feeling, a memory, or a person and place. As I got older, I began to miss a lot of things too. At the same time though, I think not everyone realizes that you can miss something and not want it back. Missing something and wanting it back aren't exclusively tied together. I miss being a kid and not having to worry about anything, but I don't want to be young again. The freedom that comes with being an adult is simply too curious.🆅🅻

When someone says something mean and it hurts you, your natural response is to try and understand why they said that. Another way to think about this though is, why are you letting their words affect how you feel? People will always talk shit. People will always be mean and not all of them will want to listen to what you have to say in response. Sometimes, you won't even have the energy or time to talk to people who say shit about you. So if you can, let it go, and don't worry about what they may have said to you. I know that's much easier said than done because I have struggled with this a lot, but you get my point.🆅🅻

CHANGING PERSPECTIVES

I once applied for a job that I felt pretty lukewarm towards, as it didn't align with the dream position I was looking for. Eventually I was offered the position, and surprisingly found myself incredibly excited by it. There was so much good in that job which I hadn't realized before. When considering a possibility, we deal with an abstraction which exists only in our minds, and it's easy to become artificially obsessed or dissatisfied. But there's no way to fully understand an opportunity until it's before you. Next time you worry about something not being quite what you want, remember to give yourself a chance to find the good inside.**MF**

Think about all the times we willingly and even excitedly introduce new problems into our lives, just to have fun. Unsolved crossword puzzles. Sudokus. Video games. Now, what if we treated the real problems in our lives — with work, with family, with relationships — just like that? Every adversity can be a puzzle ready to be navigated and solved. Sure, the stakes are higher and issues more serious, but that's precisely why we should want to tackle the adversity head-on.**DB**

The concept of AQ has maybe changed my mindset more than any lecture or class. It's not IQ or EQ, but rather adversity quotient. The idea is that we stumble into dozens of adversities every day — large and small — from the moment we wake up and find out we forgot to charge our phone overnight, to then missing our bus, to possibly even getting into a fight with a friend. How we respond to these dozens of adversities every day is like a conditioned response, and so depending on our AQ, we may always tend to recoil and try to avoid the adversity altogether, or we may jump right into the challenge, seeing it for what it is — another of many temporary roadblocks — and even take it as an opportunity for something better (e.g. the fight with the friend will force us to finally talk about the things that we'd been neglecting all those weeks). Here's the cool thing: AQ has turned out to be a pretty good indicator of "success" and "happiness" on many levels. Here's the even cooler thing: your AQ, unlike IQ, is easily learnable and can be improved! It's a form of resilience and grit, which we all can get better at with the right mindset.⦿

One night in January, a friend and I debated taking a few days off to explore Iceland in the winter. We were weary of spending too much money, but earlier that day, we had come across $200 round-trip tickets and we felt like it was an offer we couldn't turn down. Three days later we found ourselves at an airport terminal in Reykjavik, Iceland's capital, picking up a cheap rental car. To save on food, we brought along two unopened boxes of protein bars I had neglected for the past few months. It was so cold during the day that we would have to turn the heating all the way up in order to defrost our bars on the air vents. We had a long running joke that every time we had to eat a frozen protein bar, it was the "best meal we've ever had." One night when there wasn't a hostel for us to stay in, we parked our car in the empty lot of a gas station instead of staying a night in a hotel. It was just too damn expensive. Every few hours we would wake up from the cold and I would drive our little hatchback down the highway and back to warm up the inside. Many times during the trip, we would look at each other and laugh about how miserable our situation was, but looking back, it was easily one of the most fun trips I've ever been. It was great reminder that you don't always have to break the bank to have a good time traveling.⦿

Want to experience magic? Try designing placebo effects for your everyday life. It may sound strange, but I've had luck doing things like picking out a particular Snapple juice that I only consume when I'm tired as a method for staying up late. There's not much caffeine in there, but by telling myself that I only drink it when it's absolutely necessary, I've actually found some success in staying awake. Our minds are easier to trick than we sometimes let onto, and this is something we can take advantage of.⬛

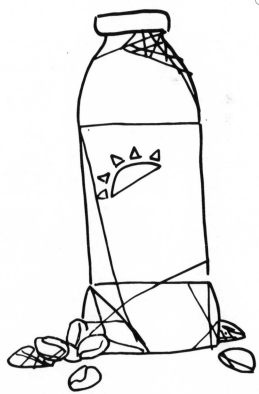

23

It's surprising what a single question can do to change an entire interaction. When you have a seemingly impossible problem and an outrageous request for someone, go up to the person and ask, "Here is what I'm struggling with right now. I know there may not be an answer, but if there were a way to solve this, what would it look like?" You might be surprised how much more excited and creative they will be in trying to help solve your problem when the stakes are low — and how this hypothetical question may just end up leading to a real solution.⬤

When you need help, ask for it. Don't let your pride get in the way. It's an understandable mistake and I know it's one that is hard to overcome. Guys especially hate to ask for help, but you should make every effort to swallow your pride and ask for it. Just like admitting that you are wrong and apologizing, it might be hard the first or second time, but once you get in the habit of it, asking for help becomes much easier.⬤

Trigger warning: sexual assault

Maybe this seems absurdly basic, but I've realized that almost everyone has completely valid reasons for their viewpoints in arguments and discussions. Even more important, just because you have a reason that is "right" doesn't mean that the other side must be "wrong." Both sides can have very valid reasons for what they believe in and it's our job to explore those different perspectives. I vividly remember having a discussion with a close friend about why all types of guns should be outlawed in America. I didn't understand why someone would go through all the training and paperwork of owning a gun simply to store it in their home all the time for self-defense reasons if they could just call the cops. Why wouldn't you just let the professionals handle it? I felt I had a compelling reason: a number of school shooters had been able to obtain a gun that one of their family owned. My friend completely agreed with me that safe gun storage was an issue, but disagreed with a ban on guns. In fact, her reasoning made me reevaluate my own views on gun control: she told me the story of how her aunt had been home alone one night and had been sexually assaulted when her house had been broken into. Her aunt had only a kitchen knife to defend herself with. Since that night, her aunt now has traumatic nightmares about that experience almost every time she falls asleep. My friend views guns as a means of self-defense and as a means of preserving and defending life. She believes that with the right training, storage, and execution of responsible gun ownership, guns can safely remain in our society without a full ban.🆅

My football coach in high school used to tell me that good, tough players weren't the ones who didn't get tackled. Everyone gets tackled; it's part of the game! Good players were the ones who got up off the ground every time they got knocked down. Sometimes, you need a hand to help get you up, and that's fine. With that said, the true testament of success in my book is how many times you can bounce back from failure.🄥🄛

I wish someone had told me earlier that to be world-class at something requires being exceptionally unique, which in turn requires having a non-traditional background. I try not to forget this. But it's important also not to confuse different with better. You always need a moral compass and the right intentions.🄓🄑

As someone once said, it's hard to be in the 99th percentile in any one thing. However, take three things that you're in the top 75th percentile in, mash them together, and tada! You're probably in the 99th percentile now.🄓🄑

CHARACTER VALUES

You gotta have enough confidence to hold your head high and be confident in yourself while having enough humility not to look down on others.

Focus on principles, not outcomes. Indeed, it's a slippery slope once we start judging our decisions and actions based on the raw outcomes. One way I've found to keep my morals in check is to ask myself, would I feel right about this if I died today and this was the last thing I did? By asking such a question, I can make sure that my answer doesn't depend on outcomes and cost-benefit calculations, but is actually aligned with the morals by which I want to live my life.**DB**

Sometimes the easiest things require the most effort. Like emptying the communal trash bin. No special skills are required to do this, and it takes minimal strength and time. But people look over it because it will not bring them recognition, they believe someone else will do it, or they do not want to lose the two minutes out of their day's plans in order to complete the task. Completing the easy things consistently really does build your character and shows others your character. If you have the self discipline and care to complete the easy things, everyone will want you to be in charge of the bigger/harder things, and they will willingly follow you.**JR**

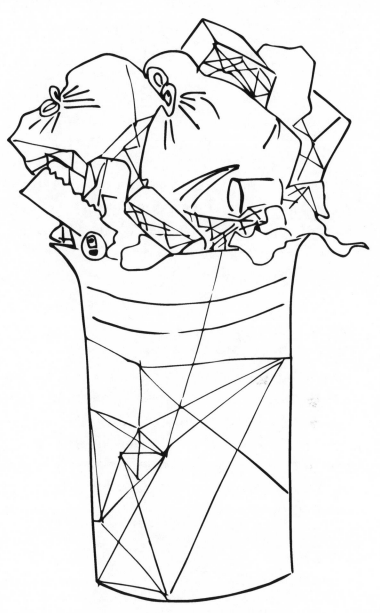

It's easier to carry extreme views than moderate views, as my friend Efe likes to say. For instance, I'm currently vegetarian for environmental reasons and have gotten rid of my smartphone for peace-of-mind reasons. Yet, the real challenge would be to realize these goals without such black-and-white lifestyle changes, finding ways to approach the problems in moderation. That takes real effort and requires mental effort to know when to do what. That said, perfect is the enemy of good, and maybe it's OK to to have black-and-white views when the alternative is to do nothing.⬤

I try to follow the principle of not starting something addictive until you have good reason to. Not that you shouldn't start, but just that you should have a thought-out reason when you do. And know that many things in life are addictive — not just drugs. Smartphones and social media and coffee are things we decided to opt into at one point in time.⬤

In high school, I struggled to find a balance between being confident in my abilities and being humble about what I had accomplished so far. I was able to find a very happy balance when I realized that I had something to learn from everyone. While I might be really good at math, someone else was much better than me in writing. You gotta have enough confidence to hold your head high and be confident in yourself while having enough humility not to look down on others.🆅🅻

I desire that every interaction I have, even the glance I give to a stranger on the subway, has compassion and meaning and will help their day even if only in the smallest way. It takes a lot of concentration and thoughtfulness to remember and live with this value at the forefront of my mind, but it has been 100% worth the effort.🅹🆁

People will drastically change over time as they grow up. Just because someone treated you badly once does not mean they will not change later on in life to become a much better person.🆅🅻

It's hard to know what kinds of days other people are having and it's very easy to form an opinion about someone you don't know based off of a short encounter. More than a few times, I've caught myself being unnecessarily snappy even though I was really just having a bad day. Don't judge others too quickly and please always remember to be kind because you never know the intricacies of someone else's lives.🅥🅛

When you're about to talk about someone else who is not present in the room, ask yourself, does this need to be said? Often the answer is no. Yet, actually listening to that voice in your head is one of the hardest things to do. I spent a week trying not to mention anything about another person — good or bad — in all my conversations. Did I succeed? No, I failed miserably. Gossip takes many forms, and this is an area I'm continually trying to get better at.🅓🅑

As Jiddu Krishnamurti said, "To observe without evaluating is the highest form of intelligence." I would only add that it may also be the highest form of kindness. The world would be a much nicer place if we could achieve even 10% of that.🅓🅑

When things go sour and you start to distrust someone, it's easy to attribute their actions to malice. This only worsens the relationship and makes them more likely and more entitled to betray you. What if instead of bringing someone closer to their negative tendencies, we gave them the benefit of the doubt, found ways to help them save face, and gave them ample opportunities to improve? Not only does this become a fun challenge to undertake, it forms the basis for a positive relationship going forward.**DB**

To really understand someone, don't just ask them what they value. Either ask them for — or even better, observe — their ranking of their values, which values compete with one another, and which ones win out and when. We can all say we value honesty and diligence, but it is only through the messiness of life and its necessary tradeoffs that our true character is revealed.**DB**

Emotions

At one point I realized I was shouting — I was angry at them, at politics, at the world — and they stopped me. They said that nothing was worth being so angry that it makes you lose control and feel hate. They were right.

Getting stuck in anger or discouragement is a dangerous place. Growth and change cannot happen if you're beating yourself up and convincing yourself that you're the worst person on the planet. Remember, the feelings of guilt and self-directed disappointment and anger are not feelings to drag you down to despair. Those feelings are simply markers to tell us that change should happen. Forgiving yourself should happen at least once a day.**JR**

Once I was in a heated argument with someone close to me about a presidential election. I looked up to this person growing up and learned many of my values from them. So at the time I was upset with who they'd voted for. It seemed like it went in the face of all I'd been taught. At one point I realized I was shouting — I was angry at them, at politics, at the world — and they stopped me. They said that nothing was worth being so angry that it makes you lose control and feel hate. They were right. I know my beliefs, and stand by them. But blind anger does nothing but damage your perspective and health.**MF**

It's easy to get caught up in your own emotions when you're discussing something you're passionate about, and it's especially easy to get frustrated when working in a team setting. I'm thinking about a specific time when a few friends and I were trying to raise money for a nonprofit to distribute medical aid in Yemen. A team member and I disagreed with how we should approach the challenge. As we continued going back and forth, we became more and more heated to the point where one of my friends then suggested we all take a quick break from the project. My friend then dragged me outside and told me to just take a few seconds to get a breath of fresh air. In these few moments, I realized that I had gotten so caught up in my own emotions that I wasn't able to see the bigger picture. We were all working together to help people in need. After a few minutes, I went back in and apologized for getting so heated. Over the next few hours, we were able to be civil and figure out a solution that worked for everyone.🆅🅛

I remember walking away from a conversation with some friends really angry because of something one of them had said to me. I thought about how I would bring it up again and what I would say. I thought about how wrong they were. I was pissed off for the entire day and when I saw them the next day, they greeted me with a smile and a hug. They had completely forgotten about what they had said and were oblivious to how it had made me feel. I did end up telling him how I felt and why I was upset, but I also realized how corrosive and damaging anger can be if you let it pool inside of you.🆅🅻

I don't get angry often, but when I do, I try to tell myself — what is anger but a feeling in my head? It then very much becomes a "me problem." Sure, there was an external event or person that triggered that anger, but why was I so taken off guard and so upset by the other's actions? Is it the result of disappointment? Miscommunication? Why did I not see this coming? What can I do to make it better for both me and the other person?🅳🅱

Life is unavoidably lonely. No one will walk the same path, think the same thoughts, or feel the same emotions as you. Love, company, and fame are ways we seek to fill the hole loneliness leaves in us, yet many achieve these things and still feel empty. Feeling understood by others can treat loneliness, but that understanding can be incredibly hard to find. Oftentimes feelings can't be communicated with words, so understanding must be demonstrated in other ways — through vulnerability, creative expression, and shared experience.🔘

The older I get, the more I realize that my flaws and fears are not unique. I used to be ashamed of myself for what I thought and how I felt, and felt terribly alone as a result. But we all experience nearly every emotion at some point in our lives. Many of the deepest connections happen when people are open about the things we all share, but never speak of.🔘

There are so many ways to spend your time. If there's something you want to do and your friends or family want to do something different, that's okay. You should do what you want even if others won't join you. I remember one family vacation in Alberta, Canada. We had gone canoeing at Lake Louise and it was an absolutely beautiful day. Behind the lake was a hike you could go on to see some glaciers. My whole family was exhausted and wanted to take a rest even though I really wanted to go on the hike. I ended up going alone anyways since it was a popular hike with a lot of foot traffic. It ended up being the perfect opportunity to step away for a little while and spend some time with my own thoughts. At the end of the hike, I managed to reunite with my very well rested family, but it was very nice to be alone to recharge. Sometimes spending time alone with yourself is exactly what you need.🆅🅻

I spent a month traveling alone, in countries whose language I didn't speak and culture I didn't understand. Twice I found myself at highway stops traveling on cheap night buses. The first time, I was the only foreigner on board. I arrived at 3am, disoriented and hungry, and tried to purchase some unfamiliar food from the dimly lit kitchens. I was only met with confused smiles, and walked back to the bus empty handed. The second time, I rode alongside a fellow traveler who spoke English. Like before, we stopped early in the morning, and were met with unfamiliar foods and unfamiliar places. But this time I felt no fear or loneliness. I was with someone who I could talk to, laugh with, and find ground in. His presence, the presence of a single connection, held back tides of uncertainty which were there before.🅜🅕

Sometimes when I do an activity with a friend that they don't enjoy, whether it be watching a movie or going on a short trip, I feel disappointed. By myself, I can experience things without worrying about other people's opinions. But companions enrich life in a way we cannot achieve alone, by providing different perspectives and creating shared memories.🅜🅕

Maybe this is just me, but it's strangely satisfying how peaceful being alone is. You can do whatever you want, whenever you want, and you don't ever have to consider what others want. The serenity of being alone is beautiful in healthy doses.🕧

Whenever I'm homesick or lonely, inundating my brain with distracting TV shows and feasting on comfort nutella only ends with me curled in a fetal position on my bed. A more effective cure that I've found is opening my window and looking at the moon. It has looked the same to me from my window at home, my window at school, and my window from many countries around the world. There is something calming and comforting knowing that the moon is the same moon during good days and bad days, from home and from a strange place. If you're searching to be re-grounded, find the small, constant thing that can help you.🕧

Your feelings are valid. Whoever you are, whatever you're going through, your feelings are valid.**MF**

Emotions aren't necessarily "good" or "bad." Those buckets exist because certain emotions make us feel things that we like or don't like. But emotions aren't signs of success or wrongdoing. They're signals from within ourselves and out in life, each telling us something different.**MF**

You are human. It's okay to make mistakes. It's okay to feel like shit. It's okay to have a meltdown and cry your emotions out. Sometimes you will just want to lay in bed and stare at the ceiling. There's nothing wrong with that and it's part of being human. Something I always try to remember is that when I reach rock-bottom, it's only a stop along the journey, not the destination. Don't fall into the trap of believing you are not destined to be happy, just because you're not where you want to be right now.**VL**

Depression is like watching the house you built burn down with you inside. After a while it's less about saving the house and more about getting out alive.

Sometimes it feels like we're below 100% for no reason, and that's okay. If you consistently run into the same problem though, digging deeper than just the present situation is an opportunity to learn more about yourself. Do you feel this way because of a deep anger? Loneliness? Unfulfilled hope? MF

Running away won't automatically solve any problems that you carry within you. But taking time away from a place that causes harm can be a necessary part of reaching a new frame of mind. MF

I've found that small actions can greatly reinforce my negative thinking. When I choose to stay in a dark room, lay down in bed, or milk my feelings with sad or angry music, it creates a self-fulfilling prophecy. MF

Suffering comes from a struggle against pain. We feel pain when experiences go beyond what we can immediatly handle, and feel suffering when we fail to flee pain. Pain is an inevitable part of life, while suffering can be avoided through accepting life's lows.🆎

When I feel low, I find myself looking for someone to save me, to show up and say something that will take the pain away, something I can't seem to come up with on my own. But the hard truth is that no one can truly save you but yourself . Little will happen without choosing to act, whether that be by reaching out to others for help or striving to heal by your own terms. That can be frightening, especially if you're tired, depressed, and see no way out. I know it has been for me. But I believe there is a strength in each of us to overcome our challenges. It just takes time.🆎

Sometimes life just isn't fair. Things don't have to go well because we want them to, and bad things can happen for no reason. Making peace with this reality is a necessary part of moving past disappointment.🆎

We are the center of our worlds, and spend most of our time thinking about ourselves. Because of this, it's easy to become hung up over past mistakes. If you find yourself overcome by embarrassment, remember that others don't dwell on your life, and that whatever you've done will most likely be forgotten.⑩

People say that I must have everything together because of how well I speak and dress. But beneath perceived confidence, I still deal with self-consciousness, anxiety, and depression at times. Everyone does. Strangers on the street, your friends, your heroes all experience some of the same struggles you feel. Without talking about it, there's no way of knowing, but it's there.⑩

We cling most tightly to parts of ourselves which we are afraid of losing or are in the process of losing. Maybe there's a good and natural reason to lose that part, and finding that reason can help with letting go.⑩

You may feel groundless and fearful in utterly new situations. This fear accompanies change, and may be impossible to avoid. But know that those feelings are temporary. You will adapt, and be all the stronger for it.🔵

When I've dealt with existential-esque crises in the past, I've usually tried one of two things to combat it:

1) Focused more on the short term (e.g. Can I find more joy doing what I'm currently doing, such as spending time with friends and family?).

2) Tried to redefine my goals in life in such a way that was favorable to how I was currently feeling (e.g. if I'm struggling academically and am not sure what I'm good at anymore, then maybe I'll try to convince myself that I'd prefer a life and career that doesn't depend on academics).

These are more than just mental tricks. They have helped me realize how much control I really can have over my own thoughts and emotions.🔵

LIVING WITH YOURSELF

When I was younger, I wanted to be cheerful and optimistic all the time regardless of how I actually felt. I thought you were supposed to tough through everything and stay the same, but I was wrong. There's nothing wrong with becoming a different person as you experience life.

Being human means making mistakes and in time you should learn to embrace this! Making mistakes is one of the best parts of life so there's really no sense in pretending that you are perfect. Our mistakes help us laugh, create memories, and learn more about ourselves and what we believe in. Mistakes make us who we are.🅥🅛

You do NOT need to have answers that will appease everyone's questions about religion. Not knowing the answer to everyone's questions about your faith does not decrease the validity of your faith or make you a worse person.🅙🅡

Our minds and bodies are constantly speaking to us, but it can be hard to notice until things go wrong. How do you physically feel right now, and what do your thoughts sound like? When have you felt this way before? If you're not sure how to listen within, throughout the day try to ask yourself "Is my body tense?", and notice how you feel. Beyond understanding oneself, listen to your gut. It tells the unspoken sum of your present and past experiences.🅜🅕

It's almost impossible for any one person to be amazing at everything they do. Most often, when someone is really good at one thing, they are probably pretty bad at something else since they've spent so much time honing in on one skill. Very few professional athletes know how to manage their money and one of my friend's dad was a great businessman, but a pretty bad father. For myself, I have spent so much time trying to achieve my own personal goals that I have not been the older brother I want to be. Most days, talking to my younger brothers over the phone is awkward at best, but I am slowly making progress. I've realized that I can't have it all and it's made me think a lot more about what I do want to devote my attention to. It's made me learn a lot about priorities. What do I value a lot and what do I value much less? Figure out your priorities and adjust how you spend your time accordingly. Over time, you may even find that you need to change priorities. That's just life.🆅🅻

Sometimes you gotta be mature enough to admit that a lot of your failed relationships are your fault. You're not gonna get them right the first few times. Even now, I still get them wrong. And hey, that's okay. Learning how to nurture a real relationship, romantic or platonic, is a part of growing up. Just keep improving and things will be alright.🆅🅻

People go through different phases as they grow up. I had a phase where I liked heavy metal music and only wanted to wear a certain brand of clothing. At one point, I spent nearly every Friday night at the mall. There will be embarrassing phases you go through as you grow older and there will be phases that you just don't want to think about. It's a part of realizing that when you're young, you're exploring the world and everything that it has to offer. I actually love to think about how much of a dork I was and still am in many respects; it makes me laugh sometimes when I'm sad and need a pick-me-up.🆅🅻

It's okay if the experiences you've gone through have changed who you are and how you see life. I used to think it was bad if you let your experiences have an impact on you. When I was younger, I wanted to be cheerful and optimistic all the time regardless of how I actually felt. I thought you were supposed to tough through everything and stay the same, but I was wrong. Your experiences are supposed to change you over time. There's nothing wrong with becoming a different person as you experience life.🆅🅻

Being patient in life is very important, especially with yourself. It'll take time to grow into who you want to be. Change doesn't happen as immediately as a lot of us would hope for; you don't just wake up one day and say "Hey I grew up." Growth is a slow process that is painful at times. You'll make mistakes and things won't always go the way you hope. Eventually though, you'll look back and realize that all this time you've been growing little by little.🆅🅻

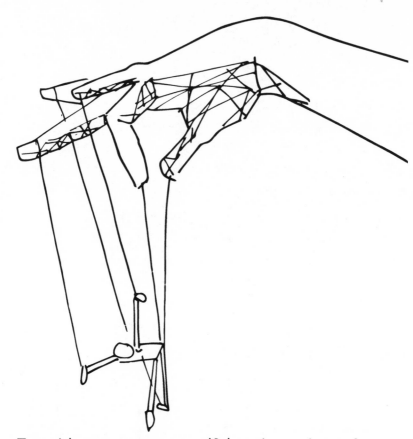

Few things are more terrifying than a loss of control. Throughout my life I've caught myself trying to control situations, the people around me, and myself, as if that would prevent things from "going wrong." So many of our actions are done in pursuit of control. We dress to control the impressions of others, we worry about missed emails and send reminders to govern the pacing of life, we read self-help books in an effort to master ourselves. While we all need some sense of control over our lives, it is equally important to learn to let go of what cannot be controlled.🔘

In our society, being selfish has a very negative image and I think people don't realize how important it is to be selfish. Sometimes, you need to put yourself first to take care of yourself mentally. To do this, it's okay to cancel a commitment, it's okay to not answer that call, it's okay to change your mind, it's okay to be alone, it's okay to take a day off, it's okay to do nothing, it's okay to speak up, and most of all it's okay to let go. Your mental health, happiness, and energy are worth prioritizing and protecting above all else. You do not owe anyone anything when you need to take care of yourself. Being selfish isn't always a bad thing. **VL**

You have your whole life to try and understand the world and the people around you. I know you're trying to solve all the world's problems, but before you try to understand everything else, understand yourself. Developing a set of values and figuring out what is important to you is crucial so that when you do venture out, you have direction and a set of beliefs to guide your decisions. **VL**

I am sometimes stupidly generous. I gave away my lunch money to friends and even carried my friend's backpack between classes daily. Sure, I was being generous, but I was not thinking about how I was being generous and how my generosity was being received. I was giving my lunch money to people who had lunch and simply wanted to eat something else, and my friend whose backpack I carried was in perfect physical condition and had no reason to not carry her own bag. I was hurting myself while not providing value for others. Generosity could be given an efficiency value — its effect and reach on others compared to the sacrifice of self. But although generosity can be given an efficiency value, I do not believe that there is a efficiency rule (such as, one should not only be generous if its efficiency surpasses a predetermined efficiency number). I believe in "being generous for generosity's sake," but it is wise to be aware of the efficiency value of one's own generous acts.🅙🅡

For most of my life, I always thought that you needed to be endlessly patient with others. If you're outside waiting to pick up a friend, it's okay if they are a little late. If you said you would meet with someone at a certain time, it's okay if they take care of other things first. If you need something from someone, but they're talking to someone else, it's okay to let them take their time. The big caveat is that these are all okay to an extent. While you should respect other people and their time, you should respect your own time too. There is a reasonable limit to how patient you can be.🆅🅻

Don't let people's opinions prevent you from doing things that will make you happy. Worry less about what others think and more about why you want to do something. There is a show from my childhood that I love watching and one of my friends asked me in passing why I still watched the show. He thought it was dumb and kind of lame. I almost stopped watching the show after he said that, but I also thought more about why I did actually watch the show after all these years. It was a great way for me to have a laugh, even if only with myself when I needed to relax and to me, that was enough of a reason.🆅🅻

"First world problems" and "rich kid problems" are problems too. Don't be a brat, but there's no need to be ashamed of your problems or to hide your difficulties.🅙🅡

There will always be a lot of pressure to change yourself to meet others' expectations. Sometimes, it'll require you to change your behavior or your clothing. Other times, it will require you to change your morals and your values. It's reasonable if the change is appropriate, but at the same time, don't give in too much. Life is far too short and precious to sacrifice who you are and what you stand for just to please others at your own expense. What makes everyone unique is the different beliefs they hold. Stay true to yourself and don't let your environment change you in a direction you're not comfortable with.🅥🅛

BECOMING A BETTER YOU

As one of my friends says, try to do one thing every day that makes you uncomfortable.

A great formula for personal growth that I borrowed from an old mentor: set a goal, write it down, tell everyone about it, go at it. Let me explain more. To achieve personal growth, you need to have some sort of goal in mind. This helps you define when you have reached some metric that you've set. A good goal might look like: I want to read a book every week or I want to wash the dishes as soon as I finish my meal. A bad goal might look like: I want to become the perfect human being. Next, writing this goal down helps make it more permanent. You can't use the excuse "I didn't remember" anymore once you've physically written your goal down. Then, tell your friends about your goal so that they can help keep you accountable when you're sitting on the couch watching Netflix. Lastly, go for it! We will never achieve of our goals if we're not willing to accept the risk of failure.🆅🅻

BECOMING A BETTER YOU

Whenever you are trying to improve at something — really trying — your path will be like a spiral that starts wide and comes to a point. You'll circle around your goal for a while, sometimes feeling that you're closer, and sometimes feeling that you've made no progress at all and just circled around. But you must believe that each effort homes the next effort a little closer to your goal. It will take much longer to get to the point than the straight line you imagined for yourself, but you must not stop putting in effort.🇯🇷

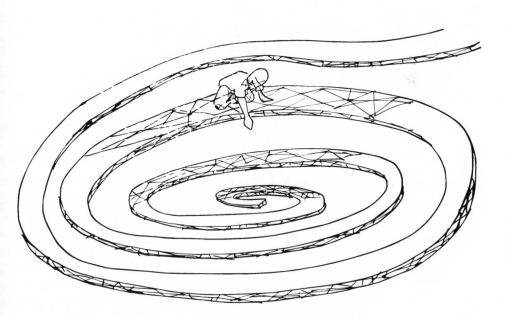

People are like giant ships that move in a particular direction with incredible inertia, continuing to do whatever we happened to do in the past. The key to steering the ship and growing ourselves is to find the rudder, i.e. the small actions that can overcome that inertia in the long run.🔵

In what ways does the "me" of a year ago exist? So many of my beliefs have changed. Nearly every cell in my body has died and been replaced. My social world has been completely rebuilt. I used to believe that over time, a new "you" is continually reborn in this way — it gave me hope that I could escape struggles I once faced. But throughout time we also carry memories and lessons which define us, guiding our thoughts and actions. It's important to recall and respect these past experiences, while knowing that they don't fully define who you'll be in the future.⚫

People don't usually change themselves; their environments do. And while we can't decide how an environment will shape us, we can decide our environment.🔵

As one of my friends says, try to do one thing every day that makes you uncomfortable.⒟⒝

I truly love traveling! For every bad experience with traveling, take two more trips — it's one of those things that gets easier and better with time and experience. Traveling is a unique situation that lets you learn about yourself and others at an accelerated pace. You learn of new cultures, and from that, you broaden your conscious knowledge of ways people can interact and expectations people can have. You learn a new form of loneliness, a new form of being the alien, and how to cope with that. You learn of new definitions of kindness and empathy. You figure out how to communicate and what is most important to communicate, and the value of each communication. And all of these learning affect your behaviors and thoughts back at home.⒥⒭

My friend was once discouraged because he often repeated other's thoughts, and concluded that this suggested a lack of critical thinking on his part. A valid argument, but I have found that whenever I regurgitated another's thoughts, I was learning and digesting their thoughts, which then quickly helped me shaped my own.⁣🅙🅡

Some people do their serious thinking in the shower. Others do it while walking. While talking. While eating. Figure out when you do your serious thinking, and then ask yourself: do you get enough of it?🅓🅑

Taking time to reflect, whether through daily journaling, lying-in-bed-recollections, or being thoughtful for a minute during lunch break, is one of the few methods that I have found to consistently result in a period of personal growth and sanity.🅙🅡

Journals are hard to keep up. I know. But what I've found helpful and more manageable is taking the time to write at a few key moments in my life. You will know when these special moments are occurring, and having the opportunity to capture those thoughts in writing can be immensely helpful both in the moment and years later.🔵

Make a mental accounting every day: How much did you consume? How much did you create? With the Internet and social media these days, it's far too easy to err on the side of consumption.🔵

The way to grow oneself is by running experiments in your life. And what is an experiment? As the author Michael Wheeler says, it's anything that is cheap and easy to reverse. Seek these opportunities out — there are many — and your life will be one of continual improvement. My experiments have included everything from using my phone less to becoming vegetarian to meeting a new person every day. Yours may be the exact opposites. It doesn't matter, as long as you're trying something new that you can learn from and undo if needed.🔵

Focus on your slope, not your
y-intercept. Where you start from in
some skill or activity doesn't matter. In
the long run, it's your pace of growth.
that will determine where you end up.◉

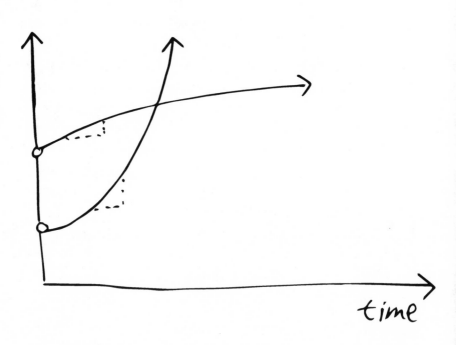

time

Just because you're introverted
doesn't mean you can't learn to be
sociable and outgoing.🅳🅱

It can be hard to incorporate new habits into
your life. I read an article somewhere that Bill
Gates sets aside 5 hours a week to read books. I
figured if someone as busy as Bill Gates could do
this, I could also find the time in my schedule. As
I started to look at how I spent my time on a day
to day basis, I found small chunks of free time that
I could be using better. At the beginning of every
day, there's always a 30 minute chunk of time in
the morning that I usually spend on my phone
drinking coffee. What a great chance to read
instead. After class when I can't be bothered to
look at another slide, I spend another 30 minutes
to catch a quick read. That's an hour a day every
week day. There's your five hours. Throw in an
hour a day on the weekends and that's 7 hours
in total. Since then, I've even finished a few books
using this strategy of making small chunks of my
free time more productive.🆅🅻

A book is the best investment you can make in yourself. Think about it. Some books explain the intricacies of entire industries. Others reflect on all the mistakes an entrepreneur made and what they would have done differently in hindsight. By reading a book, you can live through someone else's life and experience their setbacks and successes without ANY consequences. I just hope you realize how transformational reading books can be.🅥🅛

One of the most basic, and also hardest lessons, to learn in personal finance is that you should only spend when you've earned and always less than what you've earned. Debt is a vicious cycle to fall into and incredibly hard to escape without help. Maybe when you're younger, you'll have your parents' money to fall back on, but don't forget that at some point in the near future you will need to become financially independent. Probably best to start practicing now when the stakes aren't as high and in general it's just a good habit to develop at a young age.🅥🅛

FINDING YOUR PURPOSE

Maybe we don't have a purpose in life, but our own nature to fulfill.

I believe we are each guided by a life philosophy, which encompasses principles that guide our choices, as well as the assumptions beneath them. This life philosophy can be known or unconscious. A good life philosophy is complete — it can be applied throughout your life — and sound — the underlying assumptions are good and do not contradict. If a life philosophy is not complete or sound, we lose what guides us and can experience an internal crisis. Over time, we adapt our life philosophies, or recreate them in moments of crisis. What are your guiding principles? What are the assumptions they're based upon? **MF**

Maybe we don't have a purpose in life, but our own nature to fulfill. Purpose is a tangible vision, and provides a finite goal to work towards. Nature is a deep inclination which underlies one's desires, and can be pursued and expressed continuously. We tend to prioritize purpose in life, but how would you live differently if instead you focused on your nature? **MF**

One of my favorite lyrics says, "Questions of science, science and progress, could not speak as loud as my heart." Many things can motivate our path through life — family, love, ambition, and wealth to name a few. Sometimes I've soley pursued ideological goals and neglected my need for friendship and love. Other times I've done the opposite. What is driving you, and what are you driven towards? Which bring you fulfillment, and what are you missing? ⓂⒻ

"Capital" is something that creates influence, and it can come in many forms. Money, technical knowledge, and social followings are just a few types of capital. What kinds of capital do you need to reach your goals? Are there ways to reach your goals with a form of capital others don't possess, but you can see? ⓂⒻ

There are two ways to be happy: do the things that you like, or like the things that you do. ⒹⒷ

My teacher Justin taught me that it's important never to forget the money and greater forces that shape our aspirations. A job at Google is prestigious precisely because Google threw money into recruiting and publicity to make it prestigious.⏺

I have personally tried to derive my enjoyment and fulfillment not from any particular state in my life — such as having completed an assignment, attended a party, played a game — but from growth in my life — such as learning a new skill, starting a new project, building a new relationship. As Robert Louis Stevenson said, "To travel hopefully is a better thing than to arrive."⏺

When considering the impact you want to have in the world, I've found that it's often helpful to think of what Warren Buffet calls the "Ovarian Lottery": how would you want the world to be set up if you didn't yet know who you would be? In other words, you could be any one of the 7 billion people on Earth with equal likelihood, and it's a lottery of which person you become. What standards of fairness would you want in society? How would you want wealth to be distributed? And importantly, how can we get there? How can you — even just as one individual — help?⬤

Having children, becoming famous, and creating impact perpetuate our existence on earth. How many of our goals are rooted in a fear of death, and a desire to exist forever?⬤

FINDING YOUR PURPOSE

DECISION MAKING

Sometimes we focus too much on the "big" decisions and neglect the string of small decisions that will follow the big decision and arguably be even more important.

We either make decisions in life,
or live by the decisions of others.**MF**

Don't worry about getting it all right the first
time — literally no one does. No single decision
will change your life so drastically that you
cannot redirect. There are infinite paths to the
same goal — a choice is just one small step out
of many to come.**MF**

I used to treat life like a series of black-and-
white choices: this career or that career, this
activity or that activity. As time has gone on,
though, I have taken a softer, more probabilistic
approach. 80% of myself today is interested in
this, while 20% of myself is interested in that.
While it's true that we are often met with
decisions where we can only choose one, it is
also true that new information will come in and
our views will continue to evolve. By keeping
our thoughts and interest in a more flexible
framework, we can be more nimble in adapting
to changes in the future. That said, knowing
when and how to eventually commit is key.**DB**

Once I was overwhelmingly terrified of making a particular life choice. I couldn't handle the risk of making the wrong choice, so instead I let go, and decided to drift along with whatever came. I stopped worrying, but in the process I lost sight of my free will, and that was just as bad as worrying too much.**MF**

We may like to think we're the center of attention, but the truth is few people will remember our names or life stories, let alone our failures. The reason overnight successes are a thing is that people fail over and over — without anyone paying much of any attention — until one day there's a single success. Once we see failure for what is is, it's easier to take risks in our decision making.**DB**

Sometimes we focus too much on the "big" decisions and neglect the string of small decisions that will follow the big decision and arguably be even more important.**DB**

We make decisions all the time, almost every few minutes. Rarely do we ever think about how we make decisions. For the small inconsequential decisions like whether to get a medium or a large coffee, it doesn't matter as much. For larger, more serious decisions, however, the process through which you make a decision is very important. These decisions should be based on some form of information. And with that information, you have to be incredibly careful about how you collect it. Where are you getting the information from? Is there any implicit bias? Did you collect enough or too little? Making serious decisions blindly without any thought can be reckless and borderline dangerous. On the other hand, you have to be equally wary of spending too much time collecting information and analyzing it because the opportunity might pass quicker than you expected.⓿

At any big crossroads in life, our instincts are to compare the two options, hone in on the differences, and view the options as far apart as possible. But is that really the case? Why not consider the agency and choice we have in making the experiences what we desire, regardless of which option we take. In other words, as soon as we choose one option, how can we make it more like the good parts of the other? In that way, we get the best of both.🅳🅱

Whenever I'm on the verge of decision paralysis, I try to remind myself that it is a blessing that we never know the alternate paths our lives might have taken (e.g. what would have happened if I hadn't moved there or talked to that person or asked that person out?) If we did, then we'd constantly be second-guessing our decisions, knowing that there was a single right answer that we would one day figure out through our counterfactual oracle. However, because that is not the case, we will never know if our decisions are optimal or not — and that should be a huge relief!🅳🅱

DECISION MAKING

87

I've noticed that when I feel torn over a choice, it's often because my mind and heart, my logic and emotion are at odds. Both need to be aligned for you to feel confident in making a decision. If they're not, ask yourself: What am I feeling, and do I understand its root? What am I thinking, and do I need another perspective? Is there a compromise I could live with? **MF**

When I'm at a restaurant and there are too many dishes to choose from, I often split the menu in half and only pick my favorite from one side, neglecting the other side altogether. My decisions tend to be quicker this way, and I am just as happy, if not happier. **DB**

When you're having trouble making a choice, and people are a factor, really prioritize them in your decision-making. A huge part of our life, from mood to personal growth, comes from the people we're with. **MF**

Know when to throw away logic and to rely on your gut. It's not shameful to stop thinking sometimes and just make a decision. It's a skill like everything else. **DB**

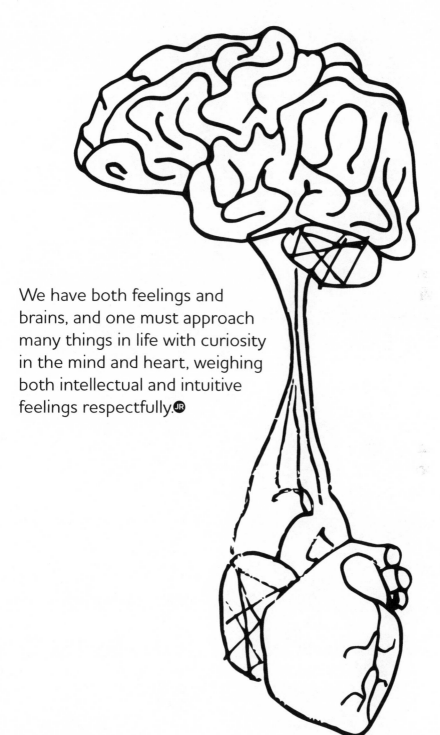

We have both feelings and brains, and one must approach many things in life with curiosity in the mind and heart, weighing both intellectual and intuitive feelings respectfully.🅹🆁

STRIVING FOR SUCCESS

Does it excite you? Do you have time for it? Do it!

STRIVING FOR SUCCESS

Action is just as important as talk, maybe even more in some cases. A lot of people like to talk about their opinions on how to make the world a better place. And why wouldn't they? Talking is so easy. It comes natural to us. We want to preach the change we want to see in hopes that we will inspire someone else to pick up the torch and actually do the work. While there will always be a time for talking, picking up the torch and doing something is how we will actually solve the world's problems.🅥🅛

If an opportunity is placed in front of you, take it with both hands. Even if you let go of it the next day, having looked at it in your hands instead of from afar can change your perspective drastically.🅜🅕

When trying to do something new and noteworthy, try asking, Why this? Why us? Why now? There are so many things one could be doing right now; why focus on this? And out of all the people out there, why are we uniquely positioned to make a difference? And finally, why hasn't this been done before? I've found that you'll seldom have perfect answers to these questions, but that the process of asking yourself them is incredibly useful nonetheless.🅓🅑

Does it excite you? Do you have time for it? Do it!🄙🄡

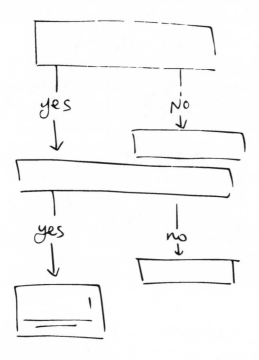

When you're making a plan, it's important to anticipate the potential problems you might face so that you are able to overcome different obstacles as they appear. At the same time, make peace with the fact that most of your plan will become obsolete when something unexpected enters the equation. When things start moving, you will need to be flexible and improvise.🅅🄛

Never let the rules tell you what you can and cannot do. Stay hungry and stay foolish. Unwritten rules and how things have been done in the past should be challenged and broken. This is the only way we create change. Don't let your past mistakes prevent you from reaching out and taking risks. If you don't fall down and scrape your knee every now and then, are you really living life? ⓥⓛ

NEVER limit yourself and your opportunities by self-intimidation. One of my biggest college regrets is not joining clubs/groups/classes because I was intimidated by the knowledge difference between myself and others on that subject. It was only after that I realized that it was common for people with zero background knowledge to join these clubs and excel past those with background knowledge. It was an opportunity missed, where I was the sole barrier.ⓙⓡ

I was an all-star kid in highschool: I had perfect grades in the hardest classes, excelled at extracurricular activities, and had numerous leadership positions. My parents told me that I could become the next famous surgeon and Mark Zuckerberg and president of the United States. These were big dreams, and I dreamed them. But it wasn't until spending a few years in college that I realized how small these dreams were. I had only been dreaming the conventional dreams, thinking about doing what has already been done. In college, I witnessed the absurd dreams, the risky dreams, the dreams that had a magnitude of the universe but no path or goal. It was those dreams that spurred me on to create unexpected but successful projects that I am now most proud of. Dream bigger than the dreams you can imagine. Take other's dreams that seem absurd, and then expand the dream taller, further outwards, and further inwards.🅙🅡

There's been more than one personal project in the past that both my friends and family were skeptical of. While that sucks, you don't always need their support to do something especially if you've looked at all the facts and decided that the project is worth doing. Sometimes you just have to trust your own judgement.🆅🅛

To succeed, you need both vision and hustle. Bold ideas are not enough if you won't put the work in to make them real. The details are as significant as the theories. Just the same, hustle without the vision is a waste of your time and energy. Consider it like a race. In a race, you run for some distance until you eventually reach a finish line. Running the race is like the hustle and the finish line is the vision. If you know where the finish line is, but don't start running, you'll never finish the race. Similarly, if you run the race, but don't know where the finish line is then you'll never finish the race either. You need to have both the hustle and the vision to finish the race.🆅🅛

As my friend and mentor John Chisholm says, passion drives perseverance, but perseverance also drives passion. Think of how the activities you enjoy can keep you up all night, but also how the things you do repeatedly can end up making you enjoy them. Focus on finding that positive feedback loop!🄳🄱

Hustle is the only way you take projects from the drawing board to real life. Most people envision these great, amazing projects and expect them to happen instantaneously. The reality of these visions is that they take an insane amount of work! So many of my friends want to build these million-dollar ventures and expect that talking around the table will do anything. If you want success, you gotta go out and earn it. It doesn't come easy and it doesn't come quickly. Great things take a lot of time and hard work to happen. Sometimes the results won't even come when you expect them to. But if you keep working, I promise you it'll be worth it. Not only just the results, but also the experience and the lessons you learn along the way.🅅🄻

Life is kind of like rowing a boat. If you don't do anything, the current of the water will take you wherever it pleases. Physically rowing the boat will take a lot of effort, but it will let you choose where to go and it will take you to your destination with enough work. Action is more important than anything else. If you have an idea, define your goals and milestones. If those seem too difficult and daunting, then break your goals down until you have small, defined milestones that you are more ready to tackle. Do something. Do anything. Get started and go. ⓥ

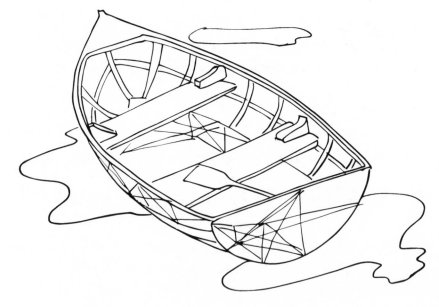

Knowing when to stop a pursuit in your life vs. knowing when to keep going with it is one of the most difficult questions out there. It's tempting to want to generalize, but I don't think there is a nice clean answer. What I do know is that it's important to at least consider the question. Too often we opt for continuing what we've done in the past without appreciating the arbitrariness by which we ended up where we did.**DB**

Finish what you start. Every single thing. Even if you fear that a half-assed finish will ruin its immaculate start: finish it. You'll build a habit of finishing, get more accomplished, and learn more from finishing something with minimal effort than not finishing it at all.**JR**

When you're grinding on a project, don't always expect immediate results. Great things take a lot of time and hard work to happen. Sometimes the results won't even come when you expect them to down the road. But if you keep working, I promise you it'll be worth it. Not only the results, but also the experience and the lessons you learn along the way.**VL**

Some people dream of becoming famous; they want to be interviewed on TV and written about in the newspapers. In high school, I was definitely one of these people and a year ago I got the chance to experience a small bit of it myself. A few friends and I had been working on a humanitarian project that got picked up by the media. The Associated Press did a story on the project and reporters from both CBS and NBC reached out to do interviews for their 6pm shows. I was eager to share the story of our cause, but also slightly excited to be on TV and on the internet. I remember thinking to myself, "Damn I made it" the moment I saw myself on TV. Over the next few days, I received emails from old mentors, calls from friends, and messages from people I didn't know congratulating me on the project. It was really exciting, but when all that died down I was surprised that I didn't really feel anything. Let me be the first to tell you. Being on TV and being on the news is not what you think it is. It honestly won't make you feel as good you would hope, and frankly, it was a little silly for me to want such a superficial thing when there are much more meaningful goals to strive for.🅥🅛

Your achievements will make you arrogant, sometimes too arrogant to ask for help when you need it, and sometimes so arrogant that others won't want to hang out with you anymore. I was lucky enough to have a mentor who caught me as I was beginning to deteriorate and she was able to steer me back on course. I hope this makes you cognisant of the risk of being too confident in yourself and when you inevitably stumble as we all do, I hope it reminds you to always be humble. Everyone needs help now and then.🄥🄛

Never forget that success is not a zero-sum thing. There is more than enough success out there, especially once you realize that your life goals are unique to you.🄓🄑

LIFE BALANCE

Doing nothing is surprisingly hard. There will always be more work to do, as work expands to any space you give it. You have to intentionally make room for rest and fun.

As my friend Jackie says, you need a balance in life, including a balance of balance and imbalance. That may sound paradoxical, but there are parts of our lives that will be imbalanced at times, and we should be willing to appreciate those parts as well.**DB**

Take a break. No responsibility. Zip. Nada. It only counts if you can wake up whenever you want to, change your entire day's activities on a whim, and ignore all responsibilities and persons. That's a real break and a necessary one.**JR**

Doing nothing is surprisingly hard. There will always be more work to do, as work expands to any space you give it. You have to intentionally make room for rest and fun.**MF**

Do not be busy in order to be lazy. You can be extraordinarily busy, but be wasting your time away. Take time to pause, to reflect, to simply observe instead of always doing. Then what you do can be a meaningful use of time and energy. **JR**

I remember not being able to celebrate one of my younger brothers' birthdays because I was "too busy." I was 16 at the time. How busy could I have actually been? I used to be so focused on thinking about my long term plan and what I wanted to be doing in a few years. You can never take back time and relive moments you missed. There will always be another time to plan out your life. Prioritize people in your life over your current work. I promise you the memories will be worth it. **VL**

In a culture of nonstop activity, I have to remind myself that it is not worth feeling guilty about the necessary daily and weekly breaks. Remember, not working like you have ten deadlines on your back and someone to impress is only normal.🇯🇷

There is a very fine line between challenging yourself and overwhelming yourself. Challenging yourself can be one of the most rewarding experiences; you'll be able to see what you are actually capable of. The line between challenging yourself and overwhelming yourself, however, is easy to accidentally cross. My freshman year in college, I wanted to challenge myself by joining clubs in different fields of study. As my extracurricular commitments grew, my schedule became more and more bogged down. I didn't have enough time to study for classes, eat, sleep, and spend an adequate amount of time for each club. I ended up eating at most 1 meal a day, sleeping 4 hours a night, nearly flunking all my classes, and half-assing my club commitments. Overwhelming yourself can be really dangerous. You'll be stressed out all the time and will find unhealthy ways to cope so it's really important that you find the right balance between challenging yourself and overwhelming yourself.🇻🇱

EFFECTIVE LEADERSHIP

When you're a leader, people look to you to make decisions. No option will ever be 100% certain, so the best you can do is make an educated choice and adapt to the consequences.

When you're a leader, people look to you to make decisions. No option will ever be 100% certain, so the best you can do is make an educated choice and adapt to the consequences.**ⓂⒻ**

I believe some of the most important qualities of a leader are to possess:
understanding — empathy towards their team and awareness of the world at large,
vision — a dream of the future few others have realized that they know how to achieve, and
urgency — a sense that things must be done now, efficiently and effectively.**ⓂⒻ**

The beautiful thing about projects and initiatives is that they can outlive the people behind them. But it doesn't happen naturally. It's never too early to start on succession planning and finding replacements.**ⒹⒷ**

Leaders need to have vision. The two are intertwined at the core. If I had to restrict a leader to only perform one task, their job would be to nurture the vision of the project. The team does not know where to go or what to do without the leader being able to point out both the short term and long term direction. Leaders need to be able to communicate the vision both to the team and the public. This helps everyone understand why the project is important. It is also the job of the leader to adjust the vision as circumstances both internally and externally change. And when necessary, the leader must protect the vision when the team gets bogged down or public favor turns, so that the project will still continue.🆅🅻

One of the most important skills you can have as a leader is being able to cut through all the crap quickly, simplify everything, and define action items. Your job as a leader is to get people going and prevent them from sitting around in a conference room discussing how to get going.🆅🅻

EFFECTIVE LEADERSHIP

I've found that a good leader is one who can walk into a room and immediately place him or herself in the shoes of the most skeptical, dissenting person there.🅓🅑

The most impactful leaders in history — whether in business or politics — weren't those who packaged and distributed products, laws, or the like. The most impactful leaders were busy spreading ideas.🅓🅑

It can be difficult to balance honesty with discretion. Leaders have a duty to be open with their team, but can find themselves in situations where it's not clear if certain info should be shared. Honesty establishes trust, while discretion can shield others from things which are truly detrimental. When trying to decide between the two, ask yourself whether you are acting selfishly — to protect yourself, to let yourself vent — or are acting in the best interest of the team.🅜🅕

Technical skills, or hard skills, can be easy to describe. By comparison, soft skills often go unappreciated and underdeveloped. Knowing things like managing conflict, empathizing with others, and leading decisions are absolutely invaluable, and it's worth both developing those skills and recognizing them in others.🅜🅕

> I value respect more than rank or position. There are too many different ways to cheat your way into rank and position. Respect on the other hand is hard won and there's often only a few ways to earn it. Rank and position you can always get back. Respect, when lost, is usually only given a second chance.🅥🅛

I like to say that I'm part of movements and quirky social trends, even when there's only two of us. Don't forget that every movement known to mankind had only a couple people on board at one point. Indeed, the second person in a movement is sometimes the most important — they're the person who decides to fully believe in something that is both crazy and not their own. If they can do it, then so can others.🅙🅡

COMMUNICATION

Honest feedback is worth its weight in gold. Surround yourself with people who can know when you are not living up to your ideals, and be sure to give them ample opportunities to let you know where you are lacking.

First figure out what you want to say. Then figure out how to say it. Don't confuse the two. **DB**

Communicating is not simply about getting your thoughts heard. It is about understanding why another's axiom is different than yours and why yours is different than theirs. **JR**

Treat every conversation like a sounding board for future conversations. Which ideas stick? Which ones don't? A conversation doesn't end with one person. Think about how you can build off those ideas in your future conversations and discover even more perspectives. **DB**

When discussing ideas, there are usually two types of conversations: creative brainstorming — where every idea is on the table — and constructive feedback — where every idea is being scrutinized. A surprising amount of conflict stems from people being confused about which of the two they're currently engaging in. **DB**

Make listening an activity, not a passive event. Listening to lectures, to friends, to family. You do not need to multitask; you will have time to listen and do other things later, but you can't turn back time to re-listen.🅙🅡

Having conversations with those who believe differently than you is as important as having conversations with those who share your faith.🅙🅡

When in large group conversations, it is easy to focus on only our own personal contributions. We try to be idea generators who insert our thoughts into the dialogue. But the rarer type of person is the one who takes a step back and tracks the conversation as a whole, regardless of his or her specific thoughts. Where is the conversation headed? Where can we as a group take it? How can I as an individual help us get there? 🅓🅑

Honest feedback is worth its weight in gold. Surround yourself with people who can know when you are not living up to your ideals, and be sure to give them ample opportunities to let you know where you are lacking.🅓🅑

COMMUNICATION

How someone seeks and accepts criticism speaks volumes about how comfortable they are with themselves, and how they see the person giving criticism.**MF**

After a conversation, I reflect on what I said and how I acted, and there is often a slight sense of embarrassment. I think of how I've stuttered, lost fluidity, or opted for filler words instead of clearly expressing myself. It feels like I have made myself more of a fool by opening my mouth. But communication through spoken language is a great gift of the human race. I often gain the courage to speak again, as well as the reminder to listen genuinely, from the quote: "Do not be ashamed of whatever you say, even if everything that you say is nothing particularly good."**JR**

Situations where you must correct another is one of the best gyms to workout self humility.**JR**

If you can't argue someone else's point better than them, then you probably don't understand it.**DB**

118

I have never encountered a situation where the best way to correct someone or point out their flaws was to do so by suggesting that they should have already been aware of their flaws and its consequences. Instead, I found that many situations and relations saved by "giving others the benefit of the doubt." Perhaps it is good to err on the gracious side and to approach gently and with no assumptions whatsoever.⓰

Approach fights as conversations, and people are less prone to become walled up in their emotions and opinions.⓰

Remember that in order to receive honest feedback, you also have to give honest feedback. Find people who you care about and help them grow in areas that they want to grow in. Identify their blind spots. But also be aware that feedback is never well taken unless properly conveyed. This is an area I've definitely been struggling with and look forward to growing in over the coming years.⓭

If you're not getting the respect you deserve in a group, be quick to start a conversation about it. And remember, having a conversation is not being self-centered or attention-seeking; it is about establishing a healthy relationship. **JR**

Gossip is something I have always struggled with, so it's been helpful for me to try to consider whenever I'm sharing some information: where did that information originally come from? Then I try to ask myself: would that person want me sharing this information in this way? **DB**

"Just kidding," "I don't know," "I don't care," "It's okay" are filler phrases we use when we don't want to confront others about how we actually feel. We both know this is true because I use these all the time and so do you. It might not be easy, but being honest about how you feel is a part of growing up and creating healthy relationships with others. **VL**

Don't underestimate the art of the cold email. It may be unsolicited, but it doesn't mean you won't get a response. A catchy email written with an understanding of the recipient's interests in mind and delivered on a Monday morning (where it'll arrive at the top of the inbox) can change the course of your life. It has for me!**DB**

Hand-written notes are all the more important in this digital age. It has become virtually costless to communicate with others on the Internet and over text, making it also more difficult to demonstrate how much we care.**DB**

Do a sanity check; your method/answer/ reasoning is probably flawed.**JR**

People love to give advice, so ask! Your thoughts exist within the confines of an individual perspective, while others can provide new and unexpected ways of looking at the world. However, remember that other people's stories are not yours — they deserve to be listened to and learned from, but not wholly embraced.**MF**

FRIENDSHIP

A new friendship is usually made up just of highs, with both people being too afraid that they may provoke the other. But to undergo tension and conflict together — and to come out of it stronger than before — is the sign of a lasting friendship.

It's sometimes said that you are the average of your five best friends. That has two implications: 1) the people you choose to become close to will shape your values, for better or for worse, and 2) you will also shape their values. Sometimes we forget about the impact we have on others, which can be just as important as how they shape us.🅳🅱

Sometimes it can be difficult to relate to someone you've just met. However, each of us has many interests and possess multifaceted personalities. Because of this complexity there is always some topic over which you can both resonate. By finding topics that you both care about, it's possible to connect on some level with anyone.🅼🅵

When I first meet someone, we're both usually pretty formal, as neither wants to seem too strange. Over time each person tests the waters, relaxing as we reach a better understanding of what's safe territory. It can be scary to become more relaxed with someone. What if they judge me? What if I go too far? But don't be afraid. This process is a necessary part of developing a deeper relationship.🅼🅵

Other people are like mirrors. Every person
we interact with creates a unique "reflection"
of our personalities, causing us to feel like
an especially awkward, introspective, or silly
version of ourselves. The closest friends
are those who offer the clearest reflection,
leaving you feeling like your very best.

After having spent many years being extremely shy and quiet, I feel comfortable sharing this with you: quiet people usually have a lot to say because they spend so much time thinking. Well, why are they so quiet then? One reason is because they're afraid of how others will react to what they have to say or how people will judge them for their thoughts. With this said, be wary of trying too hard to get them to be as outgoing as you might be. Everyone takes a different amount of time to come out of their shell.🆅🅻

When someone new joins your school, dorm, work or really anything, try to grab lunch with them. If you have never been the new kid before, I can help shed a little light on this. Before I had turned eleven, I had already moved to four different states. When you get to a new school and you don't know anyone, it's easy to feel lonely. When someone comes up to you and says hi, it can literally make your day. Some of my greatest friendships started by saying hi to the new kid.🆅🅻

The strength of your friendships are not always the same as the length of those friendships. To me, the amount of effort put into a friendship is much more indicative of how strong a friendship is. I lived with a girl — let's call her "Jennifer" — in my freshman dorm and we've been friends for about 2 years now. We used to cook together every now and then, but bumping into each other in the hallway is the extent of our interactions now. Only a few months ago, I met someone named "Jamie." Even though we both have very different passions and are in different activities, we still make an effort to grab a meal every other week and catch up on each other's lives. Because of this, I consider Jamie a much closer friend even though I've been friends with Jennifer for much longer. What's even better though is that we're both mature enough to understand that we aren't able to hang out as often because we have such different schedules, not because we aren't putting enough effort into our friendship.🅥🅛

One of my best friends, M, now lives across the country and we only get a few hours-long conversation per year. Our free times rarely overlap, so the conversations usually occur during tightly constrained windows of time, such as our lunch breaks or commutes. But the conversations we have go deeper and are more honest than any of the conversations I have with friends who I see on a daily basis. It is so easy for us to get busy and miss a scheduled talk, but we stay persistent and find ways to talk. M is someone with whom I deeply connect with, and I have realized that losing a talk with her is more than losing a conversation. Our conversations refuel me, and help me reflect and better understand myself. Our conversations are some of the few times that I get to enjoy one of life's greatest pleasures: profoundly empathizing with another. Have you ever considered what you may be losing when you lose a talk with a friend? JR

I had to say bye to an amazing group of friends last year when they graduated. I was pretty sad for a few months and in the process realized that learning how to say goodbye is such an important skill we are never taught. People will come and go in your life. Sometimes goodbye is just for a few weeks and sometimes goodbye is forever. You have to learn to be okay with the fact that you won't see a lot of these people again. You gotta have the strength and love to say goodbye permanently and wish someone the best in life knowing that you'll never talk to them again.🅥🅛

Sometimes I feel like an awkward duck; it can be hard to tell your friends how much they mean to you. I remember one time blurting out to a friend something along the lines of, "Hey, I care about you." I'm laughing at how awkward it was as I'm writing this. In order to find a better way of saying the same thing without being so direct, I've found small ways to show my friends that I care a lot about them. Sometimes texting little phrases like "drive safe," "text me when you get home," "please be careful," "how was your day?," and "I'm so proud of you" can show your friends how much they mean to you. Of course, this is only one of many ways to show you care so you should do what works for you!🅥🅛

"Can you help your sibling with that?" my mom asked me. I was willing and happy to help, but I still peeled myself away from whatever I was doing very slowly. My sibling noticed, thought that I didn't care about their project, and was hurt by my apparent lack of interest. From then on, I made it a point to respond to others as promptly as I could. Responding quickly requires little extra effort and physically shows respect and love towards others. There are plenty of other small interactions that can convey a lot of meaning and love; and it is not hard to form a more loving habitual response for each of those interactions without having to go through a intense event. **JR**

Being able to remember the small details is one of the traits I value the most in my closest friends. Before my 20th birthday, a close friend had asked me if I wanted to plan anything. I had told him no since I don't like birthdays that much. When the day came, however, he surprised me at lunch with my favorite dish, Poke. I was both surprised and touched that he remembered how much I liked it given that we had only tried Poke once or twice. Through this small act, I realized that one of the best ways to show a friend how much you care is to make an effort to remember the small details. **VL**

I've always understood that in order to pass the stage of superficial acquaintanceship, I needed to share my more intimate thoughts and feelings in order to make a meaningful connection. But I did not let many of my thoughts escape my mind out of fear. I used to be scared of sharing half-baked thoughts in fear that they would get ridiculed or picked apart, and I was scared of sharing the little joys and struggles in my life in fear that it would bore others. Many people often feel this and cope/fight this fear in a different ways. I have a peculiar solution that you may also find helpful: I started viewing every listener as someone in a very strong and loving relationship. Significant others want to listen to their partner's raw unfiltered thoughts as well as the most banal thing about their day. If the person I am speaking to, has the patience and desire to listen to their significant other (in this hypothetical relationship I have placed them in), then perhaps they are genuinely excited to hear what I say too. And sometimes, this small and weird thought is all I need to open up to another and start a deep friendship.🄡

There is absolutely nothing wrong with being a little selfish to take care of yourself, but the strongest and most amazing friends also make time to help others even when they themselves are struggling. You will never be the only one struggling; people around you will always be in and out of different conflicts. Take a look at the people around you and see what you can observe. More than a few times, I have been too caught up in my own life to realize a close friend was going through a difficult time in their life. And sometimes helping someone through a difficult time can be as simple as a reassuring voice and a hug. It's not a lot on your part and can mean the world to your friends in the right circumstances.⁣🆅🅻

It's really easy for me to get caught up in my own head about the future, the unknowns, the what-ifs. A few months ago, I had been offered the chance to give a TEDx talk. Frankly, I was scared by it. I had never spoken in front of a crowd of adults with much more experience than myself. I was afraid of doing a poor job, or that they would judge me. For a week I stressed out about whether or not I should do the talk until my roommate, having sensed something was bothering me, asked me if everything was okay. Exhausted from going back and forth with myself, I sat down and explained my dilemma. Within 15 minutes of just talking, he helped me make a decision. If something scares you, go talk to someone about it. They can push back on your thoughts and challenge your reasoning. You can trust them to provide an objective second opinion because they only want the best for you. By talking with a friend about your thoughts and fears, you can laugh and cry your way through it. Your fear might not get fixed, but at the very least, it will become less isolating after you have shared it. 🆅🅛

Once I was in a terrible place, and a friend came to ask how I was doing. It was hard to open up, but I gradually did, baring my most personal feelings and fears. Their response? Awkward silence, followed by "Good luck, I can't help you." I felt frustrated, betrayed, and lonely. For a long time I despised my friend. But I've since realized that an inability to help doesn't necessarily mean that someone doesn't care about you. Not everyone has learned how to express empathy, and those experiences come with time and practice. Believing this helped erode my anger, and pushed me to become a more empathetic friend.ⓂⒻ

Comforting people is a daunting task. "What if I make them feel worse, or I seem patronizing?" Then I realized that whenever I wanted comfort from others, I did not want them to fix my problems, or even pretend that they understood what I was going through. The comfort I enjoyed the best was empathy, when someone said, "Wow, that sucks." So when comforting a friend, simply validating their troubles by being available for them is perhaps one of the most helpful things you can do.ⒿⓇ

I have to try hard to remind myself that in order to help a friend who is struggling, it's not only about listening. It's also about you yourself sharing — not because you want to steal the show, but because you want to reciprocate and share your own vulnerabilities to make the other feel more comfortable. Notably, this is not something you can wait until the last minute to do. It won't work to share all your vulnerabilities only once a friend is struggling. You need to put in the legwork upfront, finding ways to share your insecurities and make yourself accessible and approachable in every conversation.**DB**

If someone opens up to me, I've found it helpful to never interject, to ask questions directly related to what they've said, to keep the conversation about them and not about myself, and to only bring up my own experiences when they can be used to demonstrate understanding.**MF**

People don't always need advice. Sometimes all they need is a hand to hold, a tight hug, and someone willing to listen without judgement. Your friends won't always need a solution to solve their problems. Sometimes, they just need someone to vent to, someone to hear them out. I have a friend named John. He was always this super macho tough guy who didn't say much — think strong, silent type. One night after a party, I bumped into him on the roof of our fraternity house. Our roof has an amazing view of the Charles River and the Boston skyline, so I wasn't surprised to find him up there. I remember walking up to him and asking if he would mind if I sat next to him. After sitting in silence for about 20 minutes, he just started talking about some family problems he was having. Not knowing what to say, I sat back and let him talk for nearly an hour with a few words of reassurance and my arm slung around his shoulder. After he was done, he turned to look at me and said, "Hey man thanks for listening. Everyone always has something to say, but I really just wanted someone to listen to me." He slung his arm around my shoulder and we just sat there in silence for a little bit more. Damn. It might not always work out that way, but thank god I hadn't said anything dumb.🅥🅛

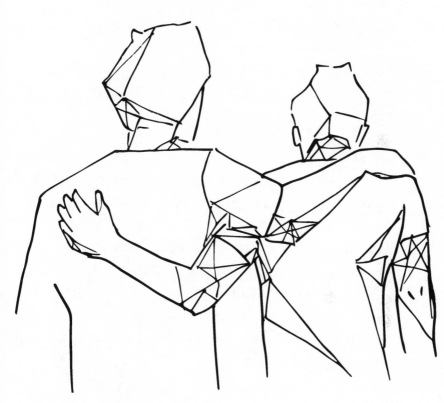

One of my friends came to me and told me he had just celebrated the Assyrian New Year. Assyrian New Year, I asked? We talked, and I learned that he was the only student at our school who identified with the ancient state of Assyria. It was his ethnicity and his culture, and one that he was exceptionally proud of. Yet no one asked him about it, and he hesitated to share it with others. Since then, I've realized how important it is to understand your friends' cultures and really let them open up about what they're truly proud of.⬤

This may be controversial, but I believe Jewish and Arab friends with a strong bond can and should be able to discuss the Israeli-Palestinian conflict with their relationship unscathed. The same goes for pro-life and pro-choice friends or Republican and Democrat friends. The hallmark of a friendship in my mind is being able to stay close no matter what is said, thought, or discussed.⬤

I think one of the signs of a strong friendship is being able to have both highs and lows together. A new friendship is usually made up just of highs, with both people being too afraid that they may provoke the other. But to undergo tension and conflict together — and to come out of it stronger than before — is the sign of a lasting friendship.⬤

I found out my good friend was the president of our college Republican Club and had voted for Trump...two days after the 2016 election. I read his name in the school newspaper. I hadn't even known we had a Republicans Club. It was that day that I realized how much we all hide from one another for fear of repercussions. But find a way to provide people with a way to share their honest views, and you'll unlock their heart and soul. One of the places I've seen this most clearly is with my friend, Efe. Although we are of different faiths (he's Muslim and I'm Jewish), we trust each other a ton. We do it by constantly asking each other questions about each other's beliefs and agreeing to disagree. Every conversation is framed as a way to open our minds to the other's point of view, regardless of what that viewpoint may be. As a result, surprises between us are rare.**DB**

For one reason or another, we tend to always focus on the one negative and not all the positives. When your friend makes a mistake and does something wrong, try not to immediately judge them based on one mistake. Everyone makes mistakes. Even if what they did was pretty bad, don't forget all the things they've done right.**VL**

FAMILY

When my dad came to visit me one day, I was surprised to see how much grey hair had begun to form on his head. I felt guilty for not giving him more of my time and attention. I had been so engrossed in my own life and forgotten that as I grow older, my dad does too.

Time passes by so quickly. Don't forget to slow down sometimes and call your family. When my dad came to visit me one day, I was surprised to see how much grey hair had begun to form on his head. I felt guilty for not giving him more of my time and attention. I had been so engrossed in my own life and forgotten that as I grow older, my dad does too. Since then, it's become a priority for me to set some time aside to check in with my family regardless of how busy I might tell myself I am.⓿

This is very personal, but losing my father has shaped me in more ways than I can imagine or even fathom. I've known nothing else in my life — how could I understand? Because he passed away before I had even turned one, it's like there's been a shadow cast in my life, a void of sorts in which I can only see the rough edges surrounding it. Many of the people that I now care about in my life knew and cared deeply about him, and vice versa. But what about me? I never really knew him. One of my biggest regrets is not digging deeper to learn more about my father and, in the process, myself. It is something I am currently working on. Sadly, it's too easy to assume that family stuff and stories will always be there... Yet, we need to make a conscious effort to uncover them.⓭⃝

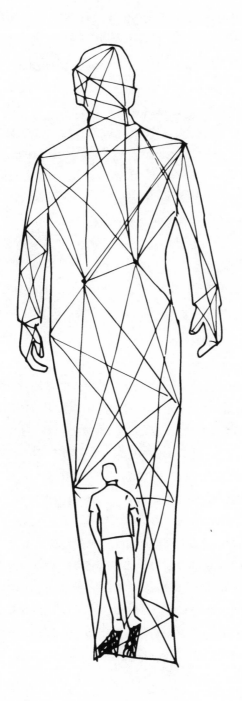

One of my biggest regrets is that I didn't find the time to truly appreciate my family while I still lived with them when I was younger. I used to speed through the food my mom made so I could get back to the game I was playing or some TV show I was watching. Now that I don't live with them, I am only able to eat my mother's food a handful of times during the year. I am also only able to see my mom and the rest of my family maybe twice a year. I sincerely wish I would have just slowed down and truly cherish the time I had with my family; I guess you really don't value what you have until it's gone.🆅🅻

We always want to take care of the people we love, but don't always think about the people who love us. A decision I regret to this day was deciding to spend one of my birthdays with a girlfriend at the time rather than with my family. In the process, I made my mom cry — I feel guilty even just writing this — and ended up splitting with that girl a few months later anyways. Such a stupid decision on my part. The people you love and the people who love you may have a lot of overlap, but they can also be two very different groups so remember to take care of both equally.🆅🅻

My favorite summer was probably the one I spent right before college, living with my grandparents in Pittsburgh. I didn't know it at the time, but my grandfather would pass away just a few months later. The moments that I now hold dearest to my heart were also some of the most mundane — grabbing groceries with them, watching tennis matches on the TV, going to the movies, and discussing my grandfather's book collection. They are mundane because they are so regular and frequent ... only until they aren't. I try to never forget that. Even the mundane — no, especially the mundane — will be the moments that you'll cherish for the rest of your life.🅑🅑

Sometimes I wish parents would better understand that spending time with your children is much more important than spending money on your children. I say this like it's very simple, but it's a little nuanced given that parents express love differently in different cultures. For example, in the traditional American culture a lot of parents might express their love verbally with "I love you" or "I'm proud of you." In the Chinese culture, however, parents express love by giving their children money to make sure they are taken care of and do not have to worry about money. Evidently, there are a number of different ways to express love, but there is a lot of value in spending time with your children and developing a strong parent-child relationship.🆅🅛

FAMILY

My Italian art teacher often ended class with some sort of maxim, such as "Call your parents; they are your friends too." But my parents raised me in a traditional authoritative manner — they were to be listened to, obeyed and respected, not friended. What did I consider a friendship and why did I not have a friendship with my parents? I defined being a friend to someone as caring for them, being interested in their life, and being present for their life joys and sorrows. Distilling friendship to this definition meant that my parents and I were friends, or at least I wanted to be friends with my parents. And if I wanted to be friends with my parents, then I should call them, and maybe even grab brunch with them.🄹🅁

The quantity of time spent together is independent and unrelated to the quality of the relationship. Nowhere have I found this to be more true than with family. As time as gone on and I've moved out of the house, my time with my parents and sister has greatly declined. Yet on almost every metric — from the breadth and depth of our interactions to how well I feel I can understand them — our relationships have only been enriched. Reflecting on this reminds me that 1) time is neither sufficient nor required for a quality relationship and 2) that we need to be intentional about how we grow our relationships.🄳🄱

When I switched back from my smartphone to a dumb phone (i.e. a $20 flip phone), I didn't realize how much that would increase my usage of phone calls. After all, what else are you going to use the phone for? I now have the opportunity to talk to my mom pretty much every day, and having that constant check-in with her has been one of the highlights of my last few years. The only thing I wish is that I had communicated more this way even when I was using a smartphone.🅳🅑

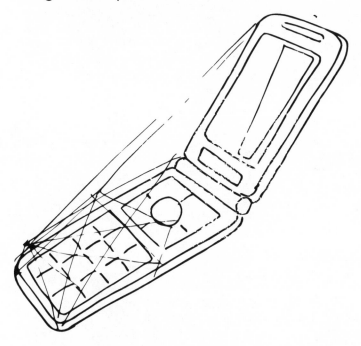

Do not be scared of acting or thinking in opposition to your parents. Value their advice, but trust in your own logic.🅙🅡

ROMANCE

As I've gotten older, I started to care less about how hot I wanted my partner to be. Instead, I started caring a lot more about finding someone who would be willing to give a relationship their time, honesty, and most importantly their effort.

What elements make up love? For me, I believe love brings understanding, comfort, and companionship which lessen the fundamental loneliness that exists in life. Love also comes with a physical attraction that sets it apart from other friendships. What do you believe love to be? If you can't put words to it, how do you think it feels? **MF**

"Anything is better than nothing" is NEVER true when looking for romantic relationships. Have standards and stick to them. Do not compromise one of your values just because that person may fulfill the rest of your values. One of the most difficult relationships is one where a single thing deeply disturbs you, but everything else is okay. **JR**

If your friends don't like someone you're dating, trust them. More often than not, they will be a better judge of a potential love interest than you will. Your friends want nothing but the best for you so they can give you an honest opinion. Another thing to remember is that your feelings will cloud ability to think clearly and prevent you from seeing the truth. **VL**

From someone who has been in a relationship where my partner was only partially invested, it sucks. If you care more, you'll get hurt as your partner continues to show less and less of an interest in the relationship. If you care less, you'll feel an obligation to stay in the relationship. Neither position is pleasant. It'll be hard to convince the one who cares less to hang out. Even when you do hang out, it'll be obvious that one of you doesn't want to be there and that will only hurt the one who does care more. Being single is a lot better than being in an unfulfilling relationship with someone who doesn't want to be there.🆅🅛

As I've gotten older, I started to care less about how hot I wanted my partner to be. Instead, I started caring a lot more about finding someone who would be willing to give a relationship their time, honesty, and most importantly their effort. At some point, you should figure out what you want from a partner and which values are most important to you in a relationship. Some trait should matter more than others when it comes to what you're looking for.🆅🅛

There is a very fine line between someone you want to have a one-night stand with and someone you want to build a serious relationship with. How you walk that line is none of my business, but don't forget that it exists. You can really hurt both yourself and your "friend" by pretending that you're walking on one side of the line when you're really on the other side.🆅🅻

If you're looking for a long-term romantic relationship, figure out whether you're aligned on the things which matter to you both as soon as possible. It's important to grow and adapt for one another, but be honest with yourself on needs that won't budge.🅼🅵

Love and compatibility are not always the same thing. The two of you can love each other more than anything else in the world, but whether you are compatible or not is out of your control sometimes. There was a girl in high school whom I cared deeply for and she had told me that she felt the same way, but we just had too many differences to make the relationship work. Sometimes, loving from afar is the best option.🆅🅻

Sometimes you meet someone and the timing just isn't right. Maybe you're not mature enough or they just got out of a long relationship. Maybe you're already in a relationship and they aren't or vice versa. Maybe you're too busy or they're not looking for something as serious as you are. That's okay. These things happen. You won't always get it right and it hurts every time, but I can confidently tell you that you will meet many, many amazing people throughout your life.**VL**

To what extent do we strive to make people love us? To what extent do we strive to pour out our love onto others? While everyone wishes to be loved, it also feels wonderful to have someone you can be in love with. But relationships should be deeper than the feel-good emotions they bring. If you find yourself in love, think about whether you've fallen for a person, or just the feelings inside you.**MF**

I know how lonely it can be "waiting to find the right one" when everybody else seems so happy in their relationships, but — trust me — one day you'll look back and cherish the time you got to spend alone discovering who you are, what you like, and what you don't like. Believe it or not, you'll become part of someone else's life eventually and part ways with a time in your life when you could do whatever you wanted, whenever you wanted.🆅🅻

Sometimes at night, I wish I had someone to hold close in bed. These nights get lonely; what can you do? I think I'm ready for a relationship; my last one was almost 3 years ago. But at the same time, maybe I'm not. Time certainly isn't always the greatest indicator of being ready. I've definitely matured a lot since then and am pretty comfortable being alone, but it's so hard to tell whether you're choosing a relationship out of loneliness or actually being ready. I'd be naive to say I wasn't a little afraid of choosing a relationship out of loneliness.🆅🅻

I wish people would spend less time looking for the right person and more time trying to become a better person. You don't need someone to complete you. Just complete yourself! Grow into who you need someone else to be.

Falling in love and staying in love are different. One happens naturally and the other requires constant work. I guarantee that you'll fall in love many, many times over the years, but what is even more beautiful is being able to stay in love. One of the best parts of staying in love is building a strong relationship and finding a partner for life, someone you can share both the special and the normal moments of life. Someone who makes you smile even at your grumpiest. Someone who will challenge you to grow as a person for the better. Someone you'll be able to happily spend the rest of your life with and unconditionally support. And hey, building that kind of relationship is not easy. There is a lot of compromise. There are going to be a lot of tough conversations, but staying in love — that's something to cherish.🅥🅛

Building a relationship isn't easy. It takes time, compromise, and learning for two different people to learn all the facets of the other. A healthy relationship should naturally start with a fair amount of stress-free communication, but even the most compatible relationships require work.🅜🅕

Don't forget that most of the things that apply to your own life also apply to relationships — setting goals, seeking growth, running experiments, finding balance... The only difference is that you're now doing these as a partnership.**DB**

Everything is a balancing act in a relationship: the amount of time you spend together, the amount of influence you have on each other, how much you depend on each other. Finding the perfect equilibrium in all of these balancing acts is hard, so relationships are hard! But it is important to be able to differentiate between not finding a balance right away, and not finding.**JR**

Nothing is more important for maintaining a healthy relationship than communication. We exist in our own heads, so everything we do makes perfect sense to ourselves. But other people don't automatically share our thoughts, assumptions, and experiences. If something's right, if something's wrong, the best way to make sure you're both understood is to be truthful.**MF**

You won't always have time to talk to your partner so if you are busy, shoot a quick text that looks like "Hey I'm busy right now, but I'll call you as soon as I get the chance" instead of taking hours to give a "Sorry, I was busy" excuse. Take 5 seconds to let your partner know you're busy, but you will get back to them. It seems simple, but people do this all the time and I've learned it the hard way both after being both the sender and one receiving the "Sorry, I was busy" excuse.**VL**

When relationships feel complex and messy — as they often will — the answers often lie with the Golden Rule (treat your partner how you'd want to be treated) and placing yourself in their shoes. Empathy is something we can all return to.**DB**

Talk! All the time. About everything. Tell your partner that you like them, what's bothering you, what you want to do. If you have a constant conversation, arguing can be a conversation instead of a high-strung "you" vs "me" contest.**JR**

When I was in one of my first serious relationships, I felt like I had to do everything I could to make my partner feel happy and in the process sacrificed a lot of my own time and energy. This is so embarrassing, but I used to make her different gifts for our anniversaries and I spent a lot of time and thought trying to come up with creative little gifts. And yes, I am cringing while I write this. Admittedly, I was a little naive to prioritize her over myself. Sooner or later, the pressure to please your partner will become more present in your life, but I hope you remember to also value your own desires, dreams, values, and expectations equally. I hope that when you get in a relationship, you remember not to lose yourself in the process of giving too much of yourself to someone else. Amazing relationships are made up of two, equally independent individuals, not one controlling the other. Your partner should learn to respect you and what you want just as you should feel the same with them.🆅🅻

Something that I never realized about relationships until I finally got older was that a relationship shouldn't be sunshine and roses all the time. There will be times when you and your partner need to have a tough conversation that neither of you want to have. You'll both come up with reasons to avoid these types of conversations, but for the sake of the relationship, you need to have them. You'll argue and fight, but avoiding these conversations is much worse than having them. At least at the end, you'll either come out with a stronger relationship or one that is over. Something in the middle is the least desirable especially if it means that neither of you are willing to work through the subjects, decisions, and topics you might have different opinions on.🆅🅛

As I was getting closer to a girl whom I wanted to date, she confessed that she had anxiety attacks a lot. She was an amazing singer and I loved to hear her sing, but I also realized that I needed to learn more about anxiety attacks and talk to her about how I could support her if she had one. No one is perfect and when you enter a relationship with someone, you have to learn to support them through the good times and the bad. True love is learning to recognize that even though your significant other is not perfect, you have chosen to embrace them for both their highs and their lows.🆅🅛

Most people don't want to hear this, but relationships involve a lot of forgiveness. You have to accept the fact that your partner isn't perfect. They will inevitably (hopefully not purposefully) hurt you, disappoint you, and upset you. Movies like to romanticize the beautiful parts of the relationship without even hinting at the ugly parts. I've learned that the best (and sometimes the hardest) way to get through the ugly parts is to sit down and have a conversation. Communicate with your partner and try to understand them. Most importantly, learn to forgive them for being human and sometimes stumbling just as you will too.🆅🅻

The guys I grew up around were always more impressed with someone who hooked up with lots of girls every weekend than someone in a steady relationship, but I've always been the other way around. I've always been more impressed with the guy who had kept a happy relationship for years than the guy who hooked up with a different girl every weekend. Just food for thought.🆅🅻

It's natural for feelings to change over time. In the beginning of a relationship, you might be completely in love with someone. As a few months go by or maybe a few years, you might become less in love. Things change and so do people. Maybe what you thought you wanted in a partner is different now. Does it make you a bad person because your feelings changed over time? Not at all. It is not your fault if the way you feel about someone has changed as the relationship progressed. Is it bad if you don't do anything about it? That's up to you, but you should be honest with your partner. You'll only hurt both your partner and yourself by not having that discussion.🆅🅛

I used to desperately miss a relationship I once had. I would daydream about the good times, and wonder if I'd ever have something so fulfilling again. Sometimes I'd even think about whether we should get back together. But there's a reason behind the end of a relationship. Even if you can't put words to it, even if it's just a feeling, there's a reason worth understanding and acting upon. That reason can help you learn what matters to you, and what you're looking for.🅜🅕

THE WORLD WE LIVE IN

We love blaming "society" because society in this definition is some obscure group of people that you conveniently don't happen to be a part of, but we also like to forget that we are society.

Nobody knows exactly what they're doing. Everyone must learn how to live life for themselves.(MF)

When thinking about what we want to accomplish in life, it's often helpful to keep the big picture in mind. We live in artificial systems in which incentives and rewards are decided for us. College is the be-all-end-all for many students because the K-12 system is designed to make it so. Young academics publish papers and strive for citations because their superiors grant tenure based on it. But who sets these incentives, and what lies in the world outside these incentives? How can you become involved in reforming and designing new systems altogether?(DB)

"They were late because they are lazy. I was late because the bus wasn't on time." We often blame others based on their character, but forgive ourselves based on the situation we're in, rather than vice versa.(MF)

When trying to accomplish something difficult in a university or other bureaucratic setting, don't try to get people's approval. Instead, find a way to do the thing where you need as few people's approval as possible. Perhaps what you're trying to do is already achievable within the current rules, and it'll work like a charm if no one knows about it. (Of course, this doesn't mean you should forget about the people in the system and any constituents who may be affected. They should always come first).**DB**

Growing up, I spent weekdays in a white rural town, and weekends with my ethnic community. I was isolated in school, and felt removed from others in my community. As a result, I developed little sense of belonging to any particular culture. I believe this provided me with an independence and impartiality which I like. At the same time, I think we all want a sense of belonging — a ground we can come to with others when everything else is uncertain. Belonging doesn't have to come from culture — I've found a home in social communities and with friends. Do you have a group which feels like family, and if not, does that bother you? If so, changing your environment and those you are with could help. By spending time with those who fulfill you, you will ultimately find a home.**MF**

We like to blame society for anything and everything. We blame society for the polarization of the left and right. We blame society for why kids are lazier and less responsible. We blame adults for not caring enough about this problem and that problem. We love blaming "society" because society in this definition is some obscure group of people that you conveniently don't happen to be a part of, but we also like to forget that we are society. I was in a class where we talked about how to address different problems in society. We talked about police brutality, systemic racism, income inequality, all sorts of topics. What struck me the most was that a lot of people had so many smart solutions and aspirational goals, but none of them wanted to execute any of them. I remember we had talked about how a community barbecue would be a great way to bring the police and minority communities together. I was pretty excited about the idea and when I asked others if they would be interested in helping organize something, they gave me excuses. "Oh, I was just talking about the idea, I don't have the time to put into something like this." Any and all change in this world starts with you making an effort.🆅🅛

I once read an article about how a group of people defamed an important religious object. Being a part of that religion, I was distraught over this event. I ran to my group of friends and explained my great distress, but to my shock, they offered no sympathy. They, my best friends who have sympathized with me over everything from family, school, and the meaning life, offered an unemotional, singular, "oh". Religion is a funny thing: it is one of the few things that people are afraid to discuss and resist sympathizing with others over. Perhaps a few questions worth ruminating on are "Are you okay with sympathizing with others when discussing their faith? Are you okay with your answer?" **JR**

We too often assume that there is a deep and intentioned reason why things are the way they are. But what if that reason is a mere quirk of history? Take our schools, which have classes separated by age, split into discrete subjects, and consisting of two-month long summer breaks. My mind was blown when I realized these were largely remnants of the 19th-century factory model for training workers — and not part of any well thought-out educational plan. **DB**

We pretend our minds are like scientists, when in reality they're closer to lawyers. Rationalization, not logic, reigns supreme in this world. Put differently: when we say we did something for so-and-so reasons, are we really being true to ourselves and others? Or did we do it for different, unstated reasons, and then just rationalize our actions after the fact?^{JR}

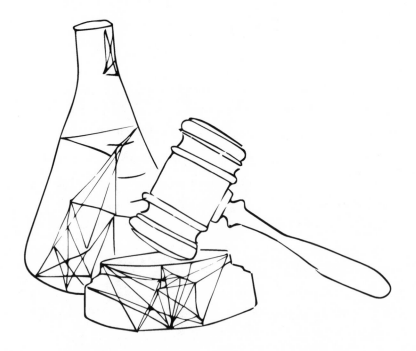

Many social conventions have no good reason behind them anymore. To get what everyone else misses, you will have to break implicit rules. Success or failure depends on which rules you break, and how you break them.🆎

If all you see are hard, serious faces, chances are everyone is reflecting the hard, serious faces they're also seeing. Smiles are an easy and infectious way to create waves of positivity in the world.🆎

At some point in the past two years, I stopped expecting anything from anyone. I had just become so fed up with anyone and everyone after being let down enough times. I could no longer count on people to return things that I let them borrow or expect people to follow up on something they said they would do. I've heard too many excuses for not being able to make a meeting or work on a project, and I've seen too many examples of someone's word that is really worth anything. Now, I'm actually relatively surprised when I meet someone who can keep their word. It's sad that this is the new standard, but for everyone reading this, keeping your word is the key to making a good impression and building a reputation of reliability.🆅🆛

Two months ago, I realized how full of crap social media was. Most people only show off the best parts of their life and they don't want to acknowledge that most of our lives are actually fairly routine and boring. Yes, even your life is boring and normal, and that's okay. There's nothing wrong with that. I wonder if some of my friends would still go out if they weren't able to post pictures of themselves in the outdoors or at some fancy restaurant with overpriced dishes. I wish we would realize sooner that happiness has nothing to do with Instagram likes and Twitter retweets.**VL**

Don't underestimate the power of defaults. Innocent until proven guilty is very different from guilty until proven innocent. This not-so-subtle distinction can be seen everywhere once you start looking.**DB**

A saying I love: You can be the juiciest peach in the world, but some people just don't like peaches.**MF**

Each of my heroes have possessed raw, harsh qualities that I only came to learn about in time. It's disappointing to learn that the ideal life of a role model doesn't exist, but it's also deeply humanizing and necessary for living a truthful life. Seek out the truth in others, and metaphorically kill the imaginary heroes in your mind.🌐

A year ago, I got the chance to meet Bill Clinton at an event. I had never met anyone famous before so I was initially very excited. When the moment came, I shook his hand and told him I really admired all the work he had done to inspire young people to make a difference in the world. We took a picture together and shared a few more words before he left to speak with some other students. He was very nice to talk to, but as I walked away, I felt a little odd. The experience was not as life changing as I had initially thought it would be. But also, what did I expect? Did it really matter that I had gotten a picture with Bill Clinton? In the grand scheme of things, not at all. Was it nice? Sure, but since then, I've realized that meeting famous people really doesn't matter as much as I once thought it would.🌐

Networking sessions may seem like one of the most regimented forms of human interaction. Because of that, networking often feels fake and carries a heartless connotation. But networking can actually be very authentic. If I approached networking with an open mind and willingness to find a genuine connection, I found others in the room reciprocated the authenticity. **JR**

My rural hometown was surrounded by forest and ocean. A day didn't go by without walls of green leaves or beautiful sunsets. Now I live in a city, and I love all the diversity, energy, and activity present. But over time, the giant grey buildings and endless seas of faces take a toll on me. When I go out to a reservation or a park, I feel refreshed and at peace. Humans were born in nature, and I believe it heals in a way nothing else can. Yet still I so infrequently visit. When was the last time you spent time in nature? How did it make you feel? **MF**

ACKNOWLEDGEMENTS

Behind every book is a story. This book began as a Google Doc started by Vick a few years ago, and then expanded from there. In addition to the four authors, we were fortunate to be joined a number of friends and supporters.

The illustrations, design, and cover artwork were done in-house by Julia Rue herself.

When it came time to editing, we recruited our friends who graciously volunteered their time. Cathy Fang, Christina Gad, Anika Gupta, Kyle Swanson, and Vivian Zhong spent countless hours marking up our words to ensure they were understood the way we wanted them to. These are people who know us well and made sure we stayed true to ourselves.

Given that we were writing this for our younger selves, we sought help from a number of high school students. Their advice and feedback was invaluable.

We want to acknowledge the countless number of people referenced in our reflections and memories. Although often left unnamed or referred to by pseudonym, they made us who we are. If someone is included in our thoughts, it's because they left an indelible mark on our lives.

Finally, to our families, for their constant love and support.

ABOUT THE AUTHORS

Vick Liu is a student at MIT passionate about creating value for others in the world. He has two inspirational younger brothers and two loving parents. He loves to find ways to make the people around him laugh and smile. In his free time, he enjoys reading interesting books, rewatching The Office, and working on personal projects like this book. One day, he hopes to experience the "overview effect" by viewing the Earth from space.

Julia Rue is a Korean-American born and raised in Southern California. She spent a quarter of her life among artists who do not prioritize a high school diploma, and the next quarter of her life in a central hub of technology where art is an alien language. These dichotomous environments strongly influenced her understanding of human nature and herself. Julia recently graduated from MIT and is currently a mechanical engineer at a product design firm, and aspires to lead her own art studio.

Mina Fahmi is a student at MIT. He is a maker at heart and enjoys creating everything from AR headsets to origami pandas. He has spent years working in tech startups and venture capital. A "child of the internet", his experiences in online subcultures along with time spent in North Africa, South America, and Asia contributed to his understanding of the world. He grew up in southern Maryland with his parents and older sister, and is looking forward to the journey after college.

Drew Bent grew up in sunny California, but his infant years were spent in New York City and may have been the most formative: he still walks quickly, folds his pizza, and puts more cream cheese than bagel on sandwiches. Other life experiences that shaped him include being raised by a single mother as a kid, biking across the country, and tutoring third graders at a community center in Cambridge. Drew majored in physics and computer science at MIT, and is now studying education reform at Stanford.

Made in the USA
San Bernardino, CA
05 December 2018